POLITICS, RELIGION AND DEATH

Memoir of a Lobbyist

Published by
The Kentucky Coalition to
Abolish the Death Penalty

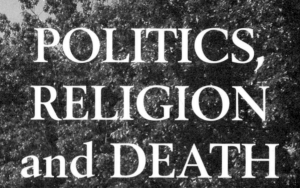

POLITICS, RELIGION and DEATH

Memoir of a Lobbyist

Carl Wedekind

ISBN 0-9786881-0-4
Library of Congress Control Number: 2006905926

Printed in Canada by Friesens Printers

For information write
The Kentucky Coalition to
Abolish the Death Penalty
P.O. Box 3092
Louisville, KY 40201-3092

www.kcadp.org

For Stephanie, and for Pat and Kaye

CONTENTS

PROLOGUE

A killing for a killing is as old as human history. It is as simple as revenge, and as complicated as fear.

After World War II, voters in Europe and England abolished the death penalty. The abolition movement spread throughout much of the world, but not in the United States. The United States government, and thirty-eight of the fifty states, hold fast to the ancient practice.

A death penalty abolition movement has started in America, it is gaining strength, and I got myself right in the middle of it.

In 1972 the United States Supreme Court in *Furman v Georgia* held that the use of the death penalty in the United States was arbitrary and capricious and therefore unconstitutional. Executions were halted throughout the country. Then in 1976 the Supreme Court in *Gregg v Georgia* held that the death penalty under new remedial statutes was constitutional. Death penalty states changed their statutes to comply with the ruling, and executions recommenced.

Kentucky was one of the death penalty states. It ceased the practice in 1972 after the Supreme Court decision and commuted the sentences of many of the men then on death row. With the new decision in 1976, Kentucky's governor called a special legislative session right before Christmas and the legislature dutifully revised the death penalty statutes and we resumed the practice. By the 1990s there were thirty-seven men on death row, some very close to the end of the line. As their numbers grew, so did opposition to the death penalty.

This is the tale of my journey with the abolition movement in Kentucky, and my reflections on our culture of violence and the interplay of politics and religion.

At the end I am still amazed at the workings of our democratic system, and by our survival, achievements, and spirituality, in spite of ourselves.

1
BEGINNING

The man whose life we were trying to save was Harold McQueen, and if ever there was a loser, it was Harold McQueen.

Harold McQueen was born prematurely to a teenager married to an alcoholic. His mother's prenatal care consisted of a visit to the doctor in the eighth month of her pregnancy, and seven pints of blood infused during labor in an effort to offset her and her baby's anemia.

Harold's school experience was limited and unrewarding. His IQ tested at 82. He was introduced to alcohol when he was ten. He was first arrested for shoplifting when he was thirteen. He joined the army and earned an "undesirable due to drugs" discharge.

Harold McQueen was labeled by a social worker as a poly-drug, chemically dependant person. He started with alcohol, learned about marijuana, heroin, and "china white" in the army, and later worked his way to speed, LSD, barbiturates and Valium.

On January 17, 1980, after an all day binge on whiskey, pot, and Valium, Harold McQueen, with his half-brother, Keith Burnel, and his girlfriend, Linda Rose, robbed a convenient store in Richmond, Kentucky. Linda Rose stayed in the car while Harold and Keith went in. They took the cash from the drawer, ripped a surveillance camera from the wall, and left the young attendant, Rebecca O'Hearn, dead on the floor from a bullet flush in her face, and another in the back of her head.

Rebecca O'Hearn was a young woman as far on the human spectrum from Harold McQueen as was possible to imagine. Her murder left devastation, grief, and fear in her family and in her community. Rebecca had just received her college degree and was working to save money for graduate school. She was intelligent, she was attractive, she was cheerful, and suddenly she was dead. There was no reason, there was no justification; there was only anger and sorrow and emptiness in those who loved her and missed her so much.

Harold McQueen was caught, convicted, and sentenced to be executed. Then his appeals started and many years followed before my participation began as he finally approached the end of the legal processes.

Harold McQueen was, of course, indigent and his appeals were handled by the Kentucky Department of Public Advocacy. One of the issues these public defenders wanted to raise was the constitutionality of execution in an electric chair. Was electrocution a tortuous death? The question was most pertinent because recently in Florida an electric chair execution culminated in the convicted man's head smoking as he roasted in the flames of his own body.

D.P.A. officials thought this could best be argued as a separate issue and they asked the American Civil Liberties Union of Kentucky if their volunteer attorneys would take it on. The man they wanted was David Friedman, the pro bono general counsel of the ACLU of Kentucky, and he agreed to take the case. David asked me if I would work with him. I was a volunteer on the ACLU legal panel at the time, so I said, of course I would, and off we went.

We had little time and we quickly dug in with research of court decisions and exploring scientific treatises on electrocution. We drafted pleadings to be filed in both federal and state courts seeking a hearing in which we would produce evidence of how the electric chair killed its victims. We really didn't know how the Kentucky electric chair would operate because it was an old handmade relic that hadn't been used for thirty-five years.

Kentucky adopted the electric chair as the method of execution at the turn of the 20th century, as had many other states, because of the increasing public aversion at this time to the horrors of hangings.

The first execution in the Kentucky electric chair was in 1911 and the honoree was Jim Buckner, a black man. When we examined the records of executions in Kentucky we found more than 50 percent of the men executed were black men, while blacks comprised less than twenty per cent of our population.

We heard many gruesome stories about death in the electric chair, but we really didn't know the facts until we researched the literature. Not much was known publicly because executions were always carried out behind closed prison doors with very few witnesses, and no pictures permitted. Little of the gore was reported in family newspapers.

The scientific literature, however, had a great deal of information. The convicted man is brought into a small room and placed in a wooden chair with leather straps binding his arms and legs. Electrodes are affixed to his shaven head and shaven right leg and his face is partially covered with a mask. When the switch is thrown, an initial charge of 2000 to 2200 volts and 7 to 12 amps are sent through his body. After a pause the voltage and amperage are lowered and reapplied at various intervals until the condemned man is dead.

The physiological studies reported that when the switch is thrown, electric current flows into the body along a restricted path, destroying all the tissue it contacts. Many vital organs remain preserved, and parts of the brain are unaffected, with continuing consciousness. The heat within the body becomes intense; eyeballs pop out; all of the muscles of the body contract with severe contortion of the limbs, fingers, toes, and face. Bodies turn bright red; there is sometimes smoke and fire, and the smell of burning flesh.

The question for the courts, is this cruel and unusual punishment within the current mores of our society? In interpreting the Eighth Amendment prohibiting cruel and unusual punishment there is the concept of "evolving decency"—recognizing that our opinions change as society changes.

We filed our suits in the Lyon Circuit Court under the

provisions of the Kentucky Constitution, and simultaneously in the United States District Court for the Western District of Kentucky under the United States Constitution. In each suit we sought court orders to halt the scheduled execution; asked for a declaration of rights; and filed a memorandum of law and facts supporting our right to a hearing. It was a lot of work.

David Friedman, our lead lawyer, was known for his acumen on civil liberties issues and his abilities as a litigator. He was an extremely nice guy, a very good friend, and we worked well together. The one difference was he really knew what he was doing while I was a retired corporate lawyer just running mightily to keep up. He was most gracious with my goofs, and there were several.

Our principal obstacle (beside some bad law and public opinion) was time. Harold McQueen's allowed appeals were coming to an end. I had time to work on the case because I was retired, but David had a full load of other cases and a family to support. We were charging ahead when, unexpectedly, we received help from Scotland.

Two young women from Glasgow landed at LaGuardia Airport in New York in early June 1997, with a mission to do summer volunteer work in the United States. They were supported by a foundation assisting students to link up with organizations opposing the death penalty. They had been given the name and telephone number of a Kentucky priest, Father Patrick Delahanty, whom they were told would help them.

They found their way to Louisville, and to Father Delahanty, and he with the help of others provided them with a place to stay. The next day Father Delahanty brought them to the ACLU office downtown and said, "Find them something to do."

Patricia Tully and Fiona Cameron had each recently graduated from the University of Glasgow where they had studied some law and become interested in and opposed to America's use of the death penalty. Almost immediately they were volunteer associate counsel in the case of *Harold McQueen v The Commonwealth of Kentucky*. They made an enormous difference.

14

There were reams of materials on the electric chair to be reviewed, countless cases to be read and briefed, affidavits to be prepared, and charts to be made for exhibits. There were documents and books to be delivered hither and yon, and they helped with all of these tasks, smiling and laughing, and teasing us about our American ways.

They were asked to read cases to resolve a procedural issue and one of the cases assigned was a class action suit by disgruntled men against a manufacturer for penile implant failures. They giggled and announced, "That is SO American!"

Their humor was broad, their faces bright and pretty, their brogue musical, and their spiritual commitment to eliminate the death penalty deep. They quickly became a joyous addition to our family.

By the end of the first week of June all of Harold McQueen's statutory appeals were exhausted, and on June 11 the governor of Kentucky, Paul Patton, signed a death warrant scheduling Harold McQueen to be executed in the electric chair after midnight and before dawn on July 1, 1997. We were running out of time.

We sought and received additional help from University of Kentucky law professor Roberta Harding, who was an expert on many death penalty issues, and from Karl Keyes, a former public defender.

There was a lot of work to be done. The pleadings were relatively simple but we had to file briefs and affidavits supporting our position both as to the law and the facts.

Here was our basic legal argument. The Eighth Amendment to the United States Constitution, part of our Bill of Rights, provides: "Excessive bail shall not be required, nor excessive fines imposed, nor cruel and unusual punishment inflicted." This last phrase was intended to insure the citizens of the new country against the experiences and history of torture in England and on the Continent.

We could not argue that the Eighth Amendment prohibited the death penalty because that punishment was prevalent before and after the adoption of the Constitution and the Bill of Rights.

There were, however, a line of cases decided over the last two hundred years establishing the test that "cruel and unusual" was to be determined by the current and evolving views of society at large. Thus, our argument was not that the death penalty was unconstitutional, but rather that putting a man to death in an electric chair was such a gruesome and tortuous affair that the conscience of society would no longer tolerate the procedure. Just as hanging had been replaced by electrocution, the latter should be replaced by a method less tortuous such as lethal injection, a method adopted by many death penalty states. We put all this in our argument as simply and as persuasively as we possibly could.

There were many strategy questions of how to avoid the impact of previous adverse court decisions; how to surmount the overriding fact that Harold McQueen already had sixteen years of court appeals; and how we could raise an entirely new issue at the very last minute. We struggled and debated and wrote and rewrote and were wise enough to always give David Friedman the final say.

I spent my professional life as a lawyer and as a businessman; I experienced team effort and camaraderie, but basically it was always a business. It was about making money. How different this was. The McQueen case was a mission. There were basically four of us working together, as much as possible during the day, mostly at night, and always on the weekend. Our affection and respect and tolerance for each other became a bond that gave us energies and insights that we otherwise would never have found. None of us would make a dime on this case, and none of us had ever been more dedicated to winning.

During the course of this none of us ever saw or met Harold McQueen. He gave us permission to act on his behalf through his counsel at D.P.A. I did get a copy of his file and some recent pictures. Harold McQueen was twenty-seven years old when he was convicted and sent to death row. He was caught once trying to make alcohol in his cell, but after that he was clean. He was, to my eye, a funny looking man: very small, about five foot five, with a mass of dark curly hair hanging down to his shoulders, and a big handlebar mustache. He never admitted his guilt in the murder. My guess was he probably couldn't remember much of what had happened.

When everything was ready to file I thought we had made one hell of a good case. We promptly served all the pleadings and briefs on the attorney general of Kentucky, counsel for the state. The circuit clerk's office in Lyon County was closed when we got there to file the papers on Friday, June 20, so we hand-delivered the documents directly to Circuit Court Judge Bill Cunningham. We sought an injunction and restraining order to stop the execution of Harold McQueen and an order setting an evidentiary hearing for us to put on proof that the electric chair caused cruel and unusual punishment prohibited by the Constitution of the United States and the Constitution of Kentucky.

Judge Cunningham took the papers home with him. Because of the seriousness of the issue and the short time period, he worked on the case most of the weekend and, to our amazement, issued his ruling on Monday.

We did not get our injunction. He would not stop the execution. His five-page opinion stated he was bound by previous Kentucky decisions upholding execution by the electric chair and he had no authority to rule whether the "evolving decency" concept should cause a change in the law. That would be up to the Kentucky Supreme Court. Then he wrote, "This is a final and interlocutory order subject to immediate appeal...if [the Kentucky Supreme Court] wishes to have the opportunity to revisit this issue and even reverse its previous holding, it may simply reverse this order, enjoin the July 1, 1997 electrocution of the Plaintiff, and remand it to this court for further proceedings."

We lost, but not entirely. Judge Cunningham made it possible for us to go immediately to the Kentucky Supreme Court and seek our relief. We started work on the appeal.

Then we were interrupted.

When we delivered our state court case to Judge Cunningham we also filed our similar federal case in the United

States District Court for the Western District of Kentucky and the case was assigned to federal judge Thomas B. Russell. To our enormous surprise we received notice from the federal court clerk on Tuesday, June 24, that Judge Russell had entered an Order in our case.

What was the decision? The opinion and order of the federal district judge was faxed to us. We read, we looked at each other— we WON! The federal district judge ordered the warden at the Kentucky State Penitentiary to stop the execution.

The four of us read and reread the opinion and order, and whooped, and laughed, and cried. Here was the main part of the decision:

"...the Eighth Amendment's prohibition against cruel and unusual punishment is required to be interpreted in a 'flexible and dynamic manner' and measured against 'the evolving standards of decency that mark the progress of a maturing society' *Gregg v. Georgia*. Therefore, whether an action presents 'cruel and unusual punishment' may change as time progresses, i.e., what may have been considered by society to be an acceptable punishment in 1897, or even 1987, may be different in 1997. With respect to this case, the fact that only six jurisdictions in the United States now use electrocution as the sole means of execution may be an indication of society's evolving intolerance for this particular means of execution.

"...the Court shall enjoin the July 1, 1997, execution pending an appeal of this order and, if affirmed, pending an expedited hearing on the merits of plaintiff's Section 1983 claim."

We had accomplished what the pundits said could not be done. We had successfully raised the issue of the constitutionality of execution by the electric chair. We were exhausted. After a bit, David got up from his chair behind his desk, came around, still smiling he looked at us and said, "Okay, we have won round one. Let's prepare for round two."

We completed preparations and filed papers appealing the Lyon Circuit Court Opinion to the Kentucky Supreme Court and we received notice that the attorney general of Kentucky was appealing the federal district court decision and stay of execution to the United States Sixth Circuit Court of Appeals. Once more we ground out the pleadings and the briefs and prepared for oral arguments.

The Kentucky Supreme Court set oral arguments for Thursday, June 26, and we all went to the state capitol in Frankfort. David Friedman argued the case for Harold McQueen, before the seven justices. David Smith argued for the Attorney General and the Commonwealth of Kentucky.

David Friedman is, and looks, as sincere and forthright as any human being possibly could. He delivered our simple message of facts and law brilliantly. The state's responsive argument was all on the procedural issues. David Smith said we were too late; our case was just a delaying tactic. He said little about the merits of our case.

The questions from the judges, sitting high above us, were numerous and I furiously took notes for subsequent analysis. The questions that appeared sympathetic to our position came from Justice Janet Stumbo and Chief Justice Robert Stephens. We needed four votes and it wasn't clear where they would come from. All in all I thought the argument went very well and I was very hopeful. We had our restraining order from the federal district court, so the execution couldn't take place unless something bad happened.

Something bad happened. On Friday, June 27, the United States Sixth Circuit Court of Appeals issued a memorandum opinion and order holding that as a procedural matter the district court did not have jurisdiction over the issues raised in our case. The Kentucky attorney general won his argument that our suit was not permitted by law. The Sixth Circuit Court reversed the district court's decision to assume jurisdiction, and directed the district court to dismiss Harold McQueen's case for lack of jurisdiction, and to vacate the stay of execution.

We lost our victory. Our only hope now was the Kentucky Supreme Court and, dimly, the United States Supreme Court.

We filed papers petitioning the Sixth Circuit Court of Appeals for a rehearing on their decision. At the same time we filed a petition to the Supreme Court of the United States.

The execution was back on for Tuesday, July 1. We were running out of options. Our case was all that was left between McQueen and his execution. His other appeals were finished. If our case failed, it was over.

It was a long weekend of work and worry. We anxiously waited to hear what the Kentucky Supreme Court would do. We were in frequent contact with the office of the clerk of the United States Supreme Court as our Petition for a Writ of Certiorari was received and assigned to the justice responsible for our circuit.

On Monday, June 30, the other shoe dropped. The Kentucky Supreme Court decided against us, five to two. A summary of the court's four-page majority opinion was simply, "Appellant's claim was not timely brought."

The dissent was written by Judge Stumbo, and she said, in part:

"We (the majority) reject this possibly meritorious claim because of the time at which it was filed. Yet I believe that it is only now, with the signing by the Governor of the executive order setting the date of execution, that this claim has ripened and the right to present this particular challenge is upon us.

"We are taking this monumental step without the benefit of an evidentiary hearing. In so ruling, we abdicate the responsibility imposed upon us by our oath of office: to see that both the laws enacted by the legislature and the requirements of our Kentucky Constitution are honored in the courts of this Commonwealth.

"Something has changed in society's attitude toward the electric chair and that should be investigated. This, of course, is why today's order is so very wrong..."

Wrong or not, the order to proceed with the execution was entered, and now all that was left were the justices of the United States Supreme Court.

Monday night, June 30, a news reporter passed the word

to me that the clerk of the United States Supreme Court had announced our Petition for a Writ of Certiorari had been denied.

It was over.

The recognition of loss, of failure, settled in for all of us. I helped organize a vigil before Harold McQueen's execution on Monday night in Jefferson Square opposite the court house in downtown Louisville. I stood quietly there with several hundred others in a candlelight vigil waiting for midnight. Finally the deep resonate bells from the city hall tower reverberated through the quiet in twelve solemn tolls. The candles fluttered as from the wind of the bells.

It was quiet after the twelfth stroke, and we heard again the rhythms of the cicadas. I looked at the faces around me I could make out in the darkness. I knew many of them. Their features reflected the sadness of their thoughts. As I gazed from one to another I was overwhelmed by my own emotions. I stood in this lonely place; my body was filled with a cry—"Do not kill Harold McQueen. I am a part of what is happening. You may not do this in my name!"

Then came the realization they could, and they would. There was nothing I could do about it. This taste of powerlessness lit a flame that became a fire in my belly.

On July 1 Harold McQueen was executed in the electric chair at the Kentucky State Penitentiary at Eddyville. Harold McQueen's journey ended, and my journey as an abolitionist began.

2
—

PAUL STEVENS

Paul Stevens walked alongside Harold McQueen from his cell to the death chamber. He was Harold McQueen's closest friend. Paul Stevens was a big man, tall and slow moving. He had a large head, dark graying hair, a large nose, and deep-set eyes over high cheekbones. He didn't talk, or do anything very fast. He was what could be called a measured man. He was now 75, and this story begins in Evansville, Indiana in 1969 when Paul was 48.

Ruth and Paul Stevens had seven children: Jeff, the oldest, then Cindy, Patty, Mark, Tim, Sylvia, and Angela. Paul believed in Jesus Christ and the Catholic Church. His children, his wife Ruth, and the Catholic Church, were the basic elements of his life. He was rarely inclined to anger or to raise his voice, with family or anyone else. He relished his home, and one Saturday he counted thirty-five children in his house, a record that made him laugh and his eyes mist when he thought about it.

His twenty-year-old daughter, Cindy, was very special. He had a rarely spoken pride in being the father of such a beautiful young woman. She had a job as a private secretary, and wanted to become a social worker. She was drawn to the problems of Native Americans and had applied to work on an Indian reservation in South Dakota.

Paul worried about Cindy baby-sitting for the three little children of Lonna Jo Gatewood. He thought it was dangerous.

Paul Stevens was afraid of Jack Gatewood, Lonna's former husband. Gatewood was a drunk with a bad temper. He left home after an argument when he had beaten Lonna, and she divorced him. Now he was sought on an outstanding warrant for drawing a deadly weapon in another fight. Paul Stevens was fearful that Jack Gatewood might return to harm Lonna, and he didn't want Cindy around when that happened.

On the evening of July 10, 1969, Paul had a meeting in downtown Evansville and then stopped to visit his mother. While he was there he called home. Cindy answered the phone and he reminded her he did not want her baby-sitting for Lonna Jo Gatewood. Cindy said she had already promised she would that night but she intended to tell her it was the last time.

Close to 3 a.m. the telephone rang in the Stevens bedroom. The terror of a 3 a.m. ringing phone in a parent's bedroom is like no other. Paul Stevens picked up the phone. It was Lonna Jo's mother. She said, "Something is wrong with Cindy." Paul dressed and ran down the street. His wife, Ruth, and Mark, the middle son, got dressed and followed.

The grandmother met Paul at the door. A man lay on the rug in the living room by an overturned chair. She led Paul to the open bedroom door and he saw the body of his daughter, almost stripped of her clothes, lying in a spreading pool of blood from a wide-open slash in her chest. She was motionless.

A dream-like spell fell on Paul Stevens. He moved slowly, deliberately. He touched his daughter's cheek and knew she was dead. He saw a broken screen partly out of the window, a smashed dresser mirror on the floor, and turned back to the other room and the man on the floor. It was Jack Gatewood. He was passed-out drunk.

There were three large knives, one of them broken, on a chair beside Jack Gatewood and Paul picked each one of them up and carefully placed them out of harm's way.

An ambulance came; the medics wrapped Cindy in a sheet, placed her body on a stretcher, and slid her into the ambulance. Ruth Stevens, standing there watching, asked to go in the ambulance with her daughter, but the medics wouldn't let her. At Deaconess Hospital Cynthia Stevens was pronounced dead on arrival at 3:15 a.m.

The feel of the touch of his dead daughter's cheek dug a hole within Paul Stevens deeper and darker than anything he had ever known. It was always there. Everybody around him looked the same, but everything was different. Life faded into gray shadows. Anger and hatred were a new experience.

Two days after the murder a detective told Paul that Jack Gatewood was trying to rape Cindy when she was killed. "You know," the detective said, "You could have killed him while he was laying there. No one probably would have done a thing."

"My morals wouldn't let me do that," Paul answered.

Cynthia Stevens was put to rest in Saint Joseph Cemetery in Evansville on July 13, 1969. The eulogy at Cindy's service included her courage against her assailant's attack and Paul had part of it put on Cindy's gravestone: "My friends, my dear ones, do not weep. I fought and triumphed in God's keep."

The grand jury of Vanderburgh County met on July 17 and returned an indictment against Jack E. Gatewood charging him with murder in the first degree, punishable by life in prison or by death. Paul Stevens felt a touch of both satisfaction and anticipation penetrate the dark cloud that surrounded him.

Not long after, he was asked to a meeting in the county attorney's office to review the case against Jack Gatewood and the procedures of the criminal law that would follow. Paul assumed it was an open and shut case against Gatewood. There was no doubt of his guilt, and there was no doubt he should be executed. Paul Stevens wanted to see Jack Gatewood die. It was just too bad he couldn't die as brutally as Cindy had.

The county attorney and his assistants made a point of being considerate to Paul Stevens. He went to the meeting without Ruth who couldn't stand to listen to talk about Cindy's murder. Paul listened as they explained the procedures that would follow. He winced when the county attorney said the defense would probably seek to move the trial to another county because of local prejudice for Paul and his family. He sat quietly and listened because there was nothing else he could do.

"Mr. Stevens, I am assigning Donnie Stengel* to handle this prosecution. He is experienced, you know him, and he'll do a good job. I will be available at any time, and during the trial, to see that we do the best job possible."

Paul Stevens left. He did know Donnie Stengel and assumed he would be all right. He was disappointed the county attorney wasn't handling the case himself, but he would be a team player and help anyone get Jack Gatewood, and get him executed.

Paul met with Donnie Stengel and the detective assigned to the case. As they outlined the procedures to be followed and the evidence to be introduced, Donnie Stengel said, "Mr. Stevens, I recommend we seek a life sentence for Jack Gatewood. I don't think this is a death penalty case."

Paul Stevens stood and stared.

"What in God's name do you mean?"

"I just don't believe this is a death penalty case, and to be honest, I don't want to ask for the death penalty."

Paul Stevens picked up his creased gray hat and left without saying another word. He called the mayor of Evansville whom he knew well and explained the situation.

"I want Donnie Stengel off Cindy's case. He is against the death penalty, and if ever anyone deserved to die it is Jack Gatewood. I want him off. Will you help me?"

The mayor responded, "I understand, Paul, let me see what I can do."

Donnie Stengel was taken off the case.

The chief deputy prosecutor of Vanderburgh County, Stephen Haas, was put in charge of the prosecution and he understood it was to be tried as a death penalty case.

The passing of time from the night of Cindy's murder, day after day, made the hole of hurt and anger in Paul that much deeper. His only relief was imagining Jack Gatewood's death, and its balm lay only in shutting out the remembrance that Cindy was gone.

He could not understand how everything in the outside

*The name "Donnie Stengel" is a pseudonym.

world was the same. The steps up to the house, the door, the trees and the cars and the people were all there as if nothing had happened. How could everything be so unconscious of the change? How could the flowers, and the cracks in the walk, be so indifferent?

One Monday morning Paul Stevens went to the Whirlpool plant where he'd worked for many years. Instead of going to his office as usual, he went to the superintendent's office, and handed him his resignation. He stood there while the man read the short letter, and then the two of them stared at each other.

His boss said, "Paul, I'm sorry. I'm sorry for everything." Paul left and never went back.

Going to and from his own house became a problem. The old house, which sat back from the road, was less than a block from the neat little cottage where Cindy had been murdered. Paul couldn't bear to be near it. He began to stay mostly at home and not go out very much. He found that whiskey brought a gentle forgetfulness.

The county attorney was right about the trial being moved. Jack Gatewood hired James Lopp to defend him and his first step was to ask for a change of venue. The court agreed and the case was transferred to the city of Vincennes, on the banks of the Wabash River. From that time forward, for every hearing, every deposition, every day of the trial, Paul Stevens had to drive the 54 miles on US 41 from Evansville to the courthouse in Vincennes. It was long, it was flat, it was boring, and sometimes Paul felt it would be his undoing. But he made it every time.

When it was time Paul and Ruth went into the courtroom and Stephen Haas led them to seats in the front row directly behind the prosecuting attorney's table. The courtroom filled and another family took seats at the other end of the first row behind the defense table. Paul was told they were all Gatewoods.

At times Paul was asked to sit at the table with the prosecutor. He was eight feet from Jack Gatewood. Paul kept thinking, why doesn't he say he's sorry?

Stephen Haas kept his word and the prosecution sought

the death penalty, which made that issue a major element in the jury selection. Each potential juror on the panel was asked in the voir dire if he or she could, if the evidence warranted, vote for the death penalty.

Normally this was not much of a problem in mid-America in 1970, but early in the proceedings one of the panelists said, "I think there is too much chance for human error to take a person's life. If the error comes out later, it's too late." This apparently set a lot of folks thinking, and thereafter some sixty potential jurors had to be excused or were stricken before the jury panel was completed. The final jurors were all men, and each had given an assurance that he could render a verdict for the death penalty.

The selection of the jury took the first two days, and Paul listened to all the questions and answers, the exchanges between the lawyers and the judge, and the judge's rulings, but most of it slid easily out of his consciousness and memory. When an individual expressed reservations about the death penalty Paul dismissed their words without consideration, as simply irrelevant.

The third morning, after the highway trek, Paul and Ruth took their usual seats. Paul was particularly aware of the Gatewood family taking seats at the other end of the front row. It occurred to him they too had to get up early every morning and drive that mindless highway from Evansville. It was strange to think of them as Jack Gatewood's mother and sister. He couldn't handle it, so he turned back to watch the front of the courtroom.

The first witness was Dorothy Jeffreys whom the newspaper reporter described as "an attractive grandmother." Mrs. Jeffreys was Lonna Jo Gatewood's mother, and grandmother to the three children Cindy was babysitting. Lonna Jo and her children had moved in with her mother after the divorce and it was her house where Cindy had been murdered.

Mrs. Jeffreys testified she came home late and when she entered the house the first thing she saw was Jack Gatewood lying on the floor in the living room, apparently unconscious. He had on only his trousers and socks, and she saw a large meat hook sticking out of his belt and a knife stuck in one of his socks. She went into the children's room and they were sleeping, and then in the other bedroom she found Cindy, almost naked, lying in the bed soaked with blood. She called the police and Cindy's father. When she went back to look closely at Cindy, she seemed to be dead. As she looked around she saw two knives on a chair and a rifle with a telescopic sight behind the chair alongside a butcher knife and a T-shirt with bloodstains. She said she had never seen the rifle before. There was stuff strewn everywhere, and the place was a mess.

An investigating police officer testified he found a blood stained knife handle in front of the couch in the living room, and later found the blade inside the couch. He saw blood stains in three rooms, papers and clothes scattered on the floors, a broken lamp, and the telephone pulled from the wall in the bedroom. There was, he said, evidence of a long and terrible struggle.

The officer said he searched Jack Gatewood at the scene and found a red billfold containing $1.92 in his back pocket. That billfold was identified as Cindy Stevens'.

Jay Futreli was the next witness. He testified he and Cindy were engaged to be married and that she had called him that evening about 9:45 while she was baby-sitting. They talked about a half an hour and everything was fine at that time.

Mark Stevens, Cindy's seventeen year-old brother, was called next. He testified he knew Cindy was baby-sitting and when he got off work at midnight he decided to go keep her company. He got to the small cottage about 12:15 and it was all dark. He knocked on the door but there was no answer. He assumed she had fallen asleep. He then thought he heard something, but he didn't pay any more attention and he left and went home.

Paul Stevens clenched his fists and barely took a breath as he listened to his son tell his story. He fought with the "what ifs" in his head.

Lonna Jo Gatewood testified that her former husband, Jack Gatewood, had talked to her about getting back together. He had asked to see her the night of the murder but she decided not to, and that afternoon she left a note saying "no" in his car parked where he worked.

A final investigating police officer testified that when he examined Gatewood at the scene he saw blood on him, including on his hands and under his fingernails. In his inspection he found yet another knife in the bedroom with blood on it and the blade bent at a forty-five degree angle. He found the screen on a bedroom window had been cut open and there was a dirty footprint on the bed next to the open window. When examining the floor he had found a picture of Lonna Jo, smeared with blood, and ripped into pieces.

The officer said when Jack Gatewood came to at the scene he was told he was under arrest. He quoted Gatewood saying later, "If I done something like you said, I want to take my medicine." But Jack Gatewood denied the killing and said he didn't know Cindy Stevens.

Tests taken on Jack Gatewood's blood several hours later showed an alcohol count of .23, almost triple the statutory level for intoxication.

The coroner testified Cindy Stevens died of multiple stab wounds, and estimated the time of death at 11:45. He also noted police found a clock in the bedroom broken and stopped at 11:45.

He said his examination disclosed she had not been raped.

When the prosecution announced the conclusion of their case the judge looked at the defense table and said, "Mr. Lopp?"

The defense counsel rose and said, "Your honor, the defense will call the defendant, Mr. Jack Gatewood, to the stand."

Jack Gatewood got up amidst a very surprised crowd in the courtroom. Paul Stevens stared at him intently. He appeared to be such a nothing figure. Such a nothing person to have taken his Cindy. He was short and slight, no more than 5 foot 8, and about 135 pounds. He sort of slid to the witness stand and swore to tell the truth.

Jack Gatewood testified he went to see his ex-wife that night and when he got to the house everything was dark. He thought he heard a child cry and he tried the front door, which was open. He then went in to the bedroom where his children were and found one of them awake and frightened. He sat by the bed and quieted the child until she went back to sleep. He then got up and left the bedroom and as he walked out he was attacked. He did not know by whom, whether it was a man or woman, but they struggled and he was knocked out. When he came to he was at the police station under arrest.

He admitted that he had had "a bunch of beers," but he denied killing Cindy Stevens.

While Paul watched and listened he realized the one thing he still wanted most, that he was waiting for, was some sign from Jack Gatewood that he was sorry. He wanted some indication Jack Gatewood recognized the enormity of what he had done and was sorry. Paul Stevens now knew he was never going to get that.

The jury stayed out for eleven hours. They got their instructions and went to the jury room at 1:30 Thursday afternoon, and didn't knock on the door with a verdict until 12:30 Friday morning. Paul Stevens sat slumped in his chair most of that time.

The verdict was read: "We find the defendant, Jack Gatewood, guilty of murder in the first degree while in the commission of a rape, punishable by life in prison: and we find him guilty of murder in the second degree, punishable by fifteen to twenty-five years in the penitentiary."

The prosecutor smiled in satisfaction, and when he looked back at Paul for approval, he saw an expression of lost bewilderment. Paul was unable to take it all in. After that long wait, he could not comprehend that Jack Gatewood would continue to live.

Not long after the trial Paul told Ruth he could not tolerate living in Evansville any longer. Everything reminded him of Cindy. Ruth agreed to move and the two of them picked Dawson Springs, Kentucky, for reasons that were never too clear to them, and were not at all clear to their children.

At the turn of the twentieth century Dawson Springs was a place for the gentry to take the waters. The old resort hotel with its wooden balcony still stood downtown, although it was now vacant. It was a pleasant small town that hadn't changed much with the times. Paul and Ruth found a house in the country, but only a few minutes from town, and moved with their two youngest children. Paul found a management job with a local plastics company and Paul and Ruth joined the Resurrection Catholic Church.

The scene changed, but Paul didn't change. The deep hole was still there and a sharp bitterness was now coupled with the hate. At each Mass Paul thought about taking Communion but he was embarrassed to rise from his seat. He said to himself, hate and Jesus cannot occupy the same body. He wanted to find Jesus again, but the hate would not move.

He plodded along like this for nine years. It was a gray time that could have lasted forever. Paul Stevens needed a miracle and he was searching.

A neighborhood couple at Resurrection said they could see the inner turmoil Paul was suffering. They invited the family to join in a weekend retreat—a Cursillo—and Paul accepted.

The three-day retreat was a series of short courses on spirituality and self-discovery, interspersed with meditations and quiet time. Paul Stevens could be quiet and alone with his thoughts, and under the influence of the gathering he no longer thought about his tragedy, but rather about what the tragedy had done to him.

He thought about his hatred for Jack Gatewood and his fixation that Gatewood be killed as Cindy had been killed. During these thoughts he asked himself, how would killing Jack Gatewood help? It wouldn't bring Cindy back.

One of the rituals of the Cursillo is repetition of prayers, and during a meditation session Paul was given the phrase, "Jesus, I love you." He commenced saying this, over and over. Paul did love Jesus, and expressing his love began to lift his spirits. He felt the hatred and the bitterness and anger of all those years past begin to melt. He was shedding a terrible weight. Paul said of that weekend retreat, "I was able to get my mind together—get the terrible hate off my shoulders. I walked myself through forgiveness."

He took Communion for the first time in more than nine years.

Sometime thereafter the parish priest, Father Frank Roof, spoke to the congregation about his ministry at the Kentucky State Penitentiary at Eddyville. He described the conditions and the men there with a particular emphasis on the spiritual needs of the men on death row. At the conclusion, Father Roof, with a note of some urgency, asked that any parishioner with the time to please speak to him about volunteering to help at the prison. Paul Stevens was the first to volunteer.

On his first visit to Eddyville with Father Roof, Paul Stevens was shaken again and again by the clang of each heavy metal door that shut with such finality behind them as they made their way down the corridors and towards the cells. It sounded like doomsday.

This was the first time Paul Stevens had ever been inside a prison, and he had never really thought about it before. Here he was, a free man, looking at other men locked behind bars. He was startled that the prisoners looked so normal, like regular people.

He walked and listened as Father Roof made his rounds. They stopped frequently and Father Roof called each man by name and asked him something, or gave word from a family member on the outside. It took a long time. When a prisoner had a request, or a question that couldn't be answered, Father Roof took a small notebook and pencil from his pocket and wrote a reminder to himself. Paul Stevens watched and listened and recognized that Father Roof was the only connection to family and the outside world many of these men had.

Then they got to death row, which was set apart from the rest. There were thirty-eight men on death row and though some of them never spoke to Father Roof, they all watched and listened when he was near.

These men on death row looked just as normal to Paul Stevens as the men in the general prison population. Father Roof stopped at each individual cell and introduced Paul to the inmate.

As they exchanged greetings Paul reminded himself that this guy smiling and greeting him had committed a vicious murder, or perhaps many murders. It was hard to even think about all they may have done.

After many hours Paul Stevens and Father Roof finally left the clanging doors behind them and were out in the sunshine. Paul Stevens slumped down on a bench. He was exhausted.

For some reason he had been most comfortable during this journey when they were on death row. He did not know why, but he felt it.

As they drove home from Eddyville, Father Roof talked to Paul about the men in prison and their needs. He urged Paul to continue his visits to the prison. He thought Paul's quiet nature and slow, sure-footed goodness would appeal to these men and would help them in their struggles with their own self worth.

Paul had no hesitation in agreeing. He was now retired from work and he had the time. After a number of visits accompanying Father Roof, Paul became a volunteer chaplain, and the guards permitted him in without Father Roof. Paul now believed that anyone who sought the death penalty, as he had for Jack Gatewood, was guilty of a grievous sin in God's eyes. He hoped his prison ministry would make up for it.

It took a while for the men at Eddyville to accept Paul Stevens, and many never did. As hungry as the men were for contact with the outside world many did not know what to do with a spiritual advisor. Paul was sensitive to this, and where there was resistance he just nodded as he passed on his rounds, and did not worry about it.

Many of the men on death row came to know Paul as a trustworthy friend. He said, sometimes, "You need me, and I need you."

One of the men on death row was Harold McQueen. Harold was not really all that normal looking. He had let his hair grow, which was permitted on death row, and it hung in waves down to his shoulders, and he had a handlebar mustache. All told, he looked pretty wild. His hair was his pride, and just before he was executed, all the hair on his head was shaved off, and he was humiliated.

After Paul Stevens learned Harold McQueen had murdered Becky O'Hearn during the robbery of a convenience store he stopped at his cell on one of his visits and they talked. Paul Stevens told Harold McQueen about the murder of his own daughter, Cindy. A number of the men on the cellblock could hear him and they were quiet and listened.

When Paul finished he stood quietly outside the cell and the two men stared at each other. Harold McQueen began to cry; after a few minutes Paul Stevens continued on his rounds.

Paul Stevens recognized his growing attachment to Harold McQueen and he asked the penitentiary office if he could have more information about him. With McQueen's permission Paul was provided a copy of McQueen's file. One of the first things he saw was Harold's IQ test score—82. One background report revealed Harold McQueen's first drinking companion was his father. Harold was ten.

Harold McQueen had now been on death row for seventeen years. He sometimes talked about his experiences with drugs and the troubles they had caused him. There was something about his wild appearance and simple childlike speech that made his stories believable, and even spellbinding.

Warden Philip Parker heard from the guards about the strong effect Harold McQueen had telling about his drug experiences. He decided to experiment by having McQueen talk to selected first time drug offenders in the general prison population. The men paid attention to Harold's stories and the warden thought he might save some lives. Harold McQueen became the penitentiary's program for warning young felons of what could lie ahead if they continued with drugs.

Giving his simple talk to young prisoners also had an effect on Harold McQueen. He saw what he was doing was considered important, and he was helping people. It was the first time he could remember helping someone. He was proud of this and looked forward to being asked to talk. He had a purpose in his life.

After Paul Stevens befriended him, McQueen began to talk to him about God. Paul introduced him to the rosary. Harold McQueen had never before known the quiet comfort he felt saying the rosary. He said it over and over, often starting at five o'clock in the morning.

One day Paul Stevens brought in rosary beads he had given to Cindy Stevens on her grade school graduation, and presented them to Harold McQueen. Harold accepted the gift and began to finger the beads sitting on the edge of his cot in his cell, and for a long time he said nothing. Finally, he looked up. "Paul, can I tell Rebecca O'Hearn's family how sorry I am for what I did?"

"Yes," Paul said, "You need to get your lawyer's permission, but I believe you can. I hope you do."

On the drive back home from Eddyville late that afternoon Paul felt the last ounce of hatred for Jack Gatewood drain away. Harold McQueen seeking repentance had touched a very deep nerve. He was an old man, broken hearted over the death of his daughter, and he could finally grieve and begin to heal.

As the time for his execution approached, Harold McQueen was in the best mental, emotional, and spiritual health of his life. While his lawyers and friends were losing their minds trying to save him he was calm and collected, and ready to accept the inevitable. The thing that troubled him most was not being able to give his drug talk. He realized this was ending, and that was painful.

The Catholic Conference of Kentucky asked and received permission from the warden to bring a technician and equipment into the prison and film Harold McQueen giving one of his last talks. They wanted to use it in the Catholic Youth Program. It was filmed at a meeting in the prison sanctuary with the usual guards and new inmates. Harold McQueen told them about his life and why he was going to be executed. He asked them to think about how they wanted to end up. They were all very quiet while the guards let him back to death row.

As his execution date approached Harold McQueen was

moved from death row to a cell in the execution area. Paul asked the warden if he could visit Harold every day now, and the warden approved from six to seven every evening. During one of these visits, Harold asked Paul if he would walk with him to the electric chair the night of the execution, and, with difficulty, Paul agreed.

Just before midnight on July 1, 1997, Harold McQueen received the last rites and the warden came and said, "It is time." Paul Stevens walked on one side of Harold McQueen, the guards on the other, and they moved slowly from his cell to the death chamber. Harold was placed in the electric chair and then he opened his hand and gave Paul Stevens Cindy's rosary.

The guards prepared Harold McQueen for execution, and when they were through, the warden said, "Do you have anything to say?"

Harold, looking straight ahead, said, "I ask that Becky O'Hearn's family try to forgive me. I thank my friends for all they have tried to do and I ask them to continue to fight the death penalty."

Paul Stevens said the final prayer, which he had written around the twenty-third psalm, Harold McQueen's favorite. When he was through he said, "Harold, I love you, and I'll always miss you."

Harold's last words were, "I love you, too, father."

And then he was electrocuted.

3

"The Last Melancholy Resource"

The Kentucky Coalition to Abolish the Death Penalty began in the 1970s as the Kentucky chapter of the Southern Coalition on Jails and Prisons. Its mission was to educate the public and gain support for abolishing the death penalty. When the parent organization folded the cause was taken up by the American Civil Liberties Union of Kentucky and the Catholic Conference, although the Catholic Conference didn't then have the strong position from American bishops and the pope that has come in more recent years.

The Catholic presence was mostly in the person of a Louisville priest, Father Patrick Delahanty. This wiry little Irishman, the son of a sportswriter for the old *Louisville Times*, joined the priesthood, best I could tell, to be a social activist. It didn't take much to set off Father Pat, and social injustice did it every time.

Pat had an extended family, an aunt, uncle, and cousins, active in law and business and politics in Louisville. I had known many of them for years.

After the execution of Harold McQueen I went to see Pat and we talked about KCADP and his campaign to abolish the death penalty. I asked him if he wanted help.

He looked at me quizzically. "Yeah," he said, but I could tell he wasn't too sure. He didn't know that much about me, or what I wanted to do. Pat was used to running his own show.

I told him I was going to research the issues and the facts about the death penalty and if he needed help in the meantime to give me a call. He looked at me more puzzled than ever, and that's where we left it.

I began reading about the death penalty and about the history of violence in Kentucky starting in colonial times and moving to the present.

Frontier life in early Kentucky was full of privations, and Indian raids, but it was not a particularly violent society among the settlers. They were too busy surviving. When Kentucky's population increased dramatically, and large numbers of slaves were brought in, the violence increased. It appeared to peak in the wars of the tobacco farmers against the American Tobacco Company Trust occurring at the end of the nineteenth century.

I completed my review of the history of violence and turned to the history of the legal development of the death penalty in Kentucky. This required going back through 206 years of Kentucky criminal law. A young volunteer law student and I made our way through the annotated revised statutes back to the early 1800s, tracking each change in the death penalty statutes.

The very earliest Kentucky statutes were not included in the codifications in the regular library stacks at the law school and the student at the checkout desk told me the early books were kept separate. He looked to a side panel, took a small key off a hook, and said, "Follow me."

We went through the library, down some steps, down more steps, and to the basement. At the far end were rows of metal stacks enclosed within heavy wire fencing stretching from floor to ceiling. The young man opened the lock on the gate to the enclosure, handed me the key, and said, "There you are." The stacks were lined with the original bound volumes of Kentucky statutes.

Kentucky separated from Virginia and became the fifteenth state in the Union, by virtue of the Kentucky-Virginia Compact, on June 1, 1792. I looked through the rows of shelves until I found a volume, *The Constitution and Laws of Kentucky, 1792*. I pulled it, with its peeling leather binding, slowly and carefully from its place. The library basement within the fence enclosing the old books was nothing but metal stacks and concrete floor. There were no chairs or desks or lamps. I sat down on the floor, cross-legged, with the volume in my lap, and began the search.

Article VIII of Kentucky's first constitution provided that existing Virginia laws would remain in effect in Kentucky until altered or repealed by Kentucky's legislature. These laws included imposing the death penalty for a wide range of offenses, including murder. The adopted laws of Virginia reflected the laws of England where at times as many as two hundred crimes were punishable by death, including pick-pocketing, shoplifting, stealing turnips, and associating with gypsies.

The very first statute on criminal law I found was in the Kentucky legislature of 1798. I read it, sitting on the floor with the old volume carefully balanced on my lap, and to my amazement it was about the death penalty. Our first criminal statute provided:

"No crime, whatsoever, committed by any free person against the Commonwealth (except murder in the first degree) shall be punished by death, within the same."

All of the many death penalty offenses, save murder in the first degree, were by this statute abolished in the state of Kentucky.

The preamble to the statute read:

"WHEREAS it frequently happens that wicked and dissolute men, resigning themselves to the dominion of inordinate passions, commit violations of the lives, liberties, and property of others; and the secure enjoyment of these having principally induced men to enter into society, government would be defective in its principal purpose, were it not to restrain such criminal acts, by inflicting due punishment on those who perpetrate them; but it appears at the same time equally deducible, from the purposes of society, that a member thereof committing an inferior injury, does not wholly forfeit the protection of his fellow citizens, but after suffering punishment in proportion to his offense, is entitled to protection from all greater suffering; so that it becomes a duty in the legislature to arrange in a proper scale the crimes which it may be necessary for them to repress, and to adjust thereto a corresponding gradation of punishments. And whereas the reformation of offenders, an object highly meriting the attention of the laws, is not effected at all by capital punishments, which exterminate instead of reforming, and should be the last melancholy resource against those whose existence is become inconsistent with the safety of their fellow citizens; which also weaken the state by cutting off so many who, if reformed, might be restored sound members to society, who, even under a course of labor might be rendered useful to the community, and who would be living and long continued examples, to deter others from committing like offenses. And forasmuch as experience in all ages and countries hath shewn that cruel and sanguinary laws defeat their own purpose, by engaging the benevolence of mankind to withhold prosecutions, to smother testimony, or to listen to it with bias; and by producing in many instances total dispensation and impunity, under the names of pardon and benefit of clergy; when if the punishment were only proportioned to the injury, men would feel it their inclination, as well as their duty, to see the laws observed; for rendering crimes and punishments therefore more proportionate to each other."

The legislature of Kentucky, at its very beginning, had declared the death penalty "the last melancholy resource" of society, to be used only for the safety of the public. In those days there were no penitentiaries on the frontier that could hold murderers and protect society.

Here were the basic arguments against the death penalty set forth by the Kentucky legislature in 1798. I was joyful, and in the silence of my basement pen I raised my fist in a power salute to the ancient tomes.

My joy in the stacks was interrupted in early January by a call from Pat Delahanty. "You want to help me on a bill in the legislature?" It sounded more like a statement than a question, and there was no greeting, nor explanation.

This abruptness was Pat's way in those days, and when it was irritating I reminded myself of my own quirks, and we moved on.

I put aside the unfinished research, and said I would. It turned out the bill he was pushing had the modest title, "The Racial Justice Act." This bill grew out of a decision of the United States Supreme Court, *McCleskey v. Kemp*.

Warren McCleskey, a black man, was convicted of killing a white man in Georgia, and was sentenced to death. On appeal he asked the court to set aside the death penalty sentence because the odds were heavily and unfairly stacked against him in Georgia. His lawyers produced statistical analysis showing a person killing a white man was 4.2 times more likely to get the death penalty than a person killing a black man. This he said was discrimination based on the race of the victim, not to mention the problems in the system if the accused were black.

The Supreme Court of the United States in a five to four decision held that while the statistics may be accurate in general, McClesky couldn't show that any individual had "purposefully discriminated" against him. Generic wasn't enough, he had to show they were out to get him.

McCleskey lost and was executed. Those who thought this unfair noted that one part of the opinion stated:

"McCleskey's arguments are best presented to the legislative bodies...

"Legislatures are better qualified to weigh and evaluate the results of statistical studies in terms of their own local conditions..."

This language gave birth to campaigns to pass legislation to permit courts to consider general statistical evidence of bias to apply to an individual in a capital case. This could make for greater racial justice, and thus the name, "The Racial Justice Act."

The first such efforts were in the Congress of the United States. After several years when these efforts were unsuccessful, activists in death penalty states, such as Kentucky, took up the cause.

The Racial Justice Act proposed in Kentucky provided, in part:

"A finding that race was the basis of the decision to seek a death sentence may be established if the court finds that race was a significant factor in decisions to seek the sentence of death in the Commonwealth at the time the death sentence was sought.

"Evidence relevant to establish a finding that race was the basis of the decision to seek a death sentence may include statistical evidence or other evidence, or both, that death sentences were sought significantly more frequently...upon persons of one race than upon persons of another race."

Now it seemed to me, entering newly on this scene, this was pretty much a no-brainer, which went to show how little I knew.

There were, I came to find out, serious problems in passing this legislation in Kentucky, and, in fact, a Racial Justice Act hadn't been passed anywhere.

But here was Father Pat Delahanty, bound and determined, and we went at it. This was my first lobbying experience and I covered my ignorance and naiveté with silent attention and a willingness to help with the simplest task.

The first meeting I attended was with Pat, lay leaders, and potential House and Senate sponsors, none of whom I knew. The bill had not yet been introduced, and the discussion was an analysis of the political situation on this issue, and consideration of possible strategies. The Democrat-controlled House of Representatives was by far the more liberal, and the votes for passage of a Racial Justice Act should be there. The Speaker of the House, Jody Richards, and the chair of the House Judiciary Committee, Mike Bowling, were favorable to the cause. We should be able to go through the committee system successfully and weather the storms that might brew on the floor.

The Senate was a much different situation. The Democrats held only a narrow majority, and the overall tenor of the Senate was a growing conservatism. The leadership, however, was good.

Senate Majority Leader David Karem was with us, and the chair of the Senate Judiciary Committee, Ernesto Scorsone, was an ally. We felt we could control the movement of the bill, but could we muster the twenty votes (out of thirty-eight members) needed for a Senate majority? That was very much an unknown.

We adopted a strategy to put our initial efforts into getting over the hurdles in the Senate, and if we could accomplish that, we could win. We began the process of going over the list of Senate members, time and again.

SB 171, The Racial Justice Act, was introduced in the Senate on January 16, 1998. The chief sponsor was Senator Gerald Neal, of Louisville. He, the lobby coalition, senate leadership, and allies, mustered cosponsors: Senators Bailey, Blevins, Boswell, Bradley, Buford, Herron, Jackson, Johnson, Kafoglis, Karem, Nunnelley, Pendleton, Saunders, Scorsone, and Seum—a total of sixteen. Only four to go.

The coalition was led by Father Pat Delahanty and included Ernie Lewis and Ed Monahan from the Department of Public Advocacy; Everett Hoffman, Executive Director of the ACLU of Kentucky; Louis Coleman of the Justice Resource Center; and volunteers from The Kentucky Alliance, the NAACP, and other groups.

One or more of these groups lobbied every day, and I went to the capitol as often as I could, maybe once or twice a week. Strategy meetings were held in the mornings twice a week in a conference room in the Annex or in Senator Gerald Neal's office. The list of senators and representatives was reviewed one by one, with a notation of what commitment we had, if any, who was responsible for contacting individual legislators, who to keep after, and who to leave alone. It was a long ritual, but one that was never boring.

SB 171 was referred to the Senate Judiciary Committee. On January 28 the chairman called it for a hearing. It went smoothly. Senator Neal explained the bill, its purpose, and hopefully its effect, and the committee voted SB 171 favorably for its first reading to the calendar on the Senate floor. January 29 was the second reading, and then the floor amendments hit. Twelve amendments were filed, a few friendly, most unfriendly. The bill and all the proposed amendments were posted for a vote on Tuesday, February 3.

Everyone worked the phones, personal appointments, and hallway sessions to keep the votes already committed, to get the additional votes needed, and to defeat the unfriendly amendments. Senator Gerald Neal wanted assurance the votes were there, and he wasn't sure. On February 3 he said he wasn't ready, and no vote was taken. SB 171 was passed over and retained on the Orders of the Day for February 4.

Senator Neal was not certain it could be done and no vote was taken on February 4. SB 171 was passed over and retained on the Orders of the Day for Thursday, February 5.

Snow started falling late Wednesday night and by Thursday morning driving was difficult. I could not get to Frankfort that day but Pat Delahanty and many of the others were there. When the Senate came into session at 2:00 p.m. Senator Neal was still in a quandary about whether or not to call SB 171.

Pat Delahanty had the post of volunteer assistant to Senator Neal and as such had access to the Senate floor. He was doing what Senator Neal asked him to do until he was interrupted by Majority Leader Karem's assistant.

"Pat, David Karem says we should call SB 171 right now."

"Why," Pat responded, "are the votes there?"

"Well, I think so, but more important look who isn't here."

Senator's Karem's assistant had been counting noses and he discovered two Senators had been snowed in and were not there to vote. They were two NO votes on SB 171.

Pat went to Gerald Neal and Neal nodded his head, "Okay, here we go."

Majority Leader Karem called SB 171 and its twelve amendments for a vote and one by one the amendments were withdrawn or defeated, and SB 171, after a stirring speech by

Senator Neal, passed the Senate by a startling 22 to 12 vote.

That hurdle was cleared. There was elation.

The bill went to the House the next day and on to its Judiciary Committee. There some troubles began. Many difficult bills are assigned to the House Judiciary Committee and committee meetings and hearings often get bogged down. SB 171 was one of many bills needing attention in the committee, and unfriendly amendments surfaced.

Weeks passed and the session, limited to sixty working days, was getting close to the end.

Finally, after three weeks in committee, SB 171 was called for a hearing on March 17. The votes were there and the committee voted to pass the bill favorably on to the House floor for its first reading. After the second reading on March 18, amendments were filed.

Now there was a whole new problem at the weekly strategy session: the amendments. There could be no amendments in the House to Senate Bill 171. There would not be time to go back to the Senate to get concurrence to any amendments. Even if there were time the votes in the Senate were no longer there. We had been very lucky to get our big vote in the Senate when we did. The favorable sentiment had not held.

All our efforts now were to line up fifty-one votes needed in the House to pass SB 171 and defeat all proposed amendments.

The bill was posted for passage in the Orders of the Day for Monday, March 30, almost the last day. Five amendments were called and each was defeated. SB 171 passed the House 70 to 23. It was colossal.

There was a small ceremony in the governor's office on Thursday, April 2, when Governor Paul Patton signed the Racial Justice Act into law. Many such signings were held out in the rotunda with press and hoopla, but the governor chose to sign this bill in his office with little fanfare. The state photographer did take pictures of about fifteen of us crowded behind the governor sitting at his desk. Louis Coleman, who is a big man, came in late and stood in front of me when the picture was snapped so my presence in the picture was as small as my role in achieving the legislation.

When we were back in the hall outside the governor's office, Senator Neal announced, "I want to talk to you people," and he led us to the conference room off the House floor. After we were seated around the large mahogany table, Gerald Neal stood up and slowly looked around at each of us. His eyes glistened with excitement.

"I want to say to you, to each of you, the coalition that you put together to pass this bill was remarkable. Truly remarkable! No one thought we could do this.

"I want myself to recognize, and I want you to recognize, that if we can do this—if we can get this bill passed, which we did—there may be no limit to what we can accomplish."

He stood at the table, his fingers excitedly tapping the dark wood, and I could imagine past frustrations in his thoughts. We all smiled and nodded and then stood up and shook hands all around, and the saga of the Racial Justice Act was concluded.

4

GOD SENT YOU

I began to ruminate about the campaign to abolish the death penalty in Kentucky. As I saw it, the campaign was pretty much Pat Delahanty. He could call on a few stalwarts and the ACLU of Kentucky when he needed special help like lobbying for the Racial Justice Act, but he basically was the organization.

I thought through what I wanted to do and called Pat. We agreed to meet and talk.

We reminisced a bit about the Racial Justice Act campaign, and then he said, "Okay, what are your thoughts about abolition?"

I laid out what was going through my head. I proposed we enlarge the campaign, raise money for a staff person and an office, print pamphlets, and all the rest. He responded with some enthusiasm but it was obvious he was skeptical about the money. The Kentucky Coalition to Abolish the Death Penalty had operated for years on his volunteer efforts and a budget of a few hundred dollars from membership dues.

I had done fund raising for justice and conservation causes and I had a Rolodex file of generous local liberals. During my early days as a lawyer I was involved in Democratic politics and had some experience in local and statewide political campaigns. My research and writing on the history of violence and the death penalty in Kentucky was done, and I now had the time and the energy to go forward

I proposed I would try to raise some money and would put together a political plan of action. I already knew how I thought it could be done.

He listened to me, but didn't know me well enough to judge if I was blowing smoke. His interest was abolition, and he figured, what the hell. He egged me on, and this was the beginning of a long period of our learning from one another.

Within three weeks I raised $22,000 in cash and pledges from three families who were friends and knew about my research on the death penalty and wanted to help. They had the resources, and when I asked they responded splendidly.

I modeled the proposed political campaign on one I was involved in years earlier. I set up a timeline for opening an office, hiring a small staff, increasing coalition members, raising more money, developing a message, and getting the message to the public and the Kentucky legislators.

It was a broad flexible outline, and I thought it was doable. The goal was to bring the issues of the death penalty increasingly before the public and the Kentucky General Assembly, working toward the adoption of legislation abolishing the death penalty. If the plan was acceptable to Pat and adopted by KCADP, I was volunteering to be campaign director and work under Pat as chair of KCADP.

Pat told me the board of KCADP hadn't met very often, but it did have members from various sections of the state. They communicated through a newsletter Pat wrote and mailed as needed. He called a meeting of the board for late January 1999 at the Catholic Conference office in Frankfort and invited me to attend and present my plan. We drove the not quite one hour drive from Louisville to Frankfort together. It was cold and clear, and as we rode we talked.

Pat had a short, laconic style of somewhat gruff statements and questions, and at one point he said to me, "You're a Presbyterian, aren't you?"

"Well, yes and no," I replied. "I went to the Presbyterian Church and to Sunday school as a kid. This was before the war and college and that stuff."

Pat nodded, and said he thought he'd heard that I was a Presbyterian.

"Well, that's just the beginning," I said. I didn't think it quite fair to leave it at that, so I went on.

"Pat, spirituality has been an evolving experience for me. There are at least two truths in the world. We don't know how life began, and we know we're going to die. Religions that have evolved tell us how it began and that we're not going to die. When it comes to this dogma, I've become an agnostic."

He said, "That's fine."

I had no idea what that meant.

Pat, it seemed to me, joined the priesthood to do service. I was not sure how he was on saving souls. What I saw was a complicated man with a driving need to help people who really needed help. And this is what he did, without wasting too much time either worrying about the Catholic Church or suffering fools gladly.

The Catholic Conference office was in a small subdivision just outside the state capitol. The Church's social policies and lobbying was directed from here.

The office was typical—a two story brick building with a middle front door, and double stairs to the second floor, that made the offices on both sides much smaller than they need be.

To the left of the front entrance was a conference room with a large table, chairs, and a TV. Here were gathered the members of the KCADP board, meeting for the first time in a good while.

Pat had few social skills. He grunted, "Hi there," to those sitting at the table with no attempt at introductions. I nodded my head at these folks, found my way back to a small pantry and got coffee, then sat at the table a couple of seats from the others.

A few more people came in and sat down and exchanged pleasantries, and then Pat said, "Well, I guess we can get started."

He explained that the KCADP bylaws required regular board meetings, and since there had not been a meeting for some time they needed to elect officers and ratify whatever had been done over the years. This was done and Pat was reelected chair.

Then he said, "Our other reason for meeting is that Carl is here to present a plan for a political campaign. He has just finished a book about the death penalty and he has become very interested in the abolition movement since Harold McQueen's execution."

With that he stopped and looked at me, as did the other six members of the board. I did not know any of these people other than one person from Louisville. I thought two of them were probably nuns, but they didn't have on their habits, and it was hard to tell.

I told them briefly about my background, my involvement with Harold McQueen, and the research and writing I had done. I watched their faces as I told my story, and if they felt any connection to what I was saying it didn't show. I told them I admired the work they had done for abolition and I believed it was time to take the next major step in the campaign.

I paused and handed out a brief outline of a political campaign, starting now and leading up to the next legislative session. It listed what we would do month by month: opening an office, hiring staff, preparing pamphlets, increasing coalition membership, calling on legislators, preparing a bill, and presumably on to a successful conclusion.

I waited while they scanned the handout, looking at the front and then the back, and going back and forth. You could see them getting more in to it and studying what was proposed.

After a few minutes, even though some were still examining the paper, I said, "This is an outline of something I believe we can do, but I need to know what you think."

A tall slender man I later learned was from Northern Kentucky near Cincinnati looked up from the paper, turning it back and forth. "This is a tall order. It would be nice to do all these things, but it's going to take money. We don't have any money. Where's the money coming from?"

A woman on my side of the table looked towards me and said, "I think this would be just fine, if we could do it. And I guess I agree; the biggest problem will be the money."

I replied, "If you all think this plan makes sense and you approve it, I believe we can raise the money."

They began to talk among themselves about some of the things they had done over the past years and comparing them with my proposal, and the tall thin guy said, "You're going to be campaign director? You got time to do that?"

"If you approve this, and want me to, the answer is yes. I've talked a good bit with Pat about the proposal and we believe it can be done."

They proceeded to talk back and forth and there seemed to be no more questions and so I interrupted them and said, "Okay, let's talk a little more about money. You are quite right that the plans do require money and in fact our initial budget is $75,000 for the first year's expenses.

"We start off with some advantages, and some good luck. While I was researching and writing about the death penalty some friends who strongly oppose the death penalty talked to me about the project and said they would help when the time came. Several weeks ago I met with them and went over this campaign outline and told them we now needed their help. They were true to their word."

As I finished saying this I brought an envelope from my pocket, opened it, and took three checks out and held them.

"I have here our first contributions, and they total $16,000 in cash and a pledge of $5,000, for a total of $21,000 to start the campaign."

I handed the three checks to Mary Lou Houck sitting to my right, the just reelected KCADP treasurer, and the one person I knew.

There was not a sound in the room. Everyone's eyes followed the three checks from my hand to Mary Lou's and rested there while she looked at the amounts. No one moved an inch.

One of the women sitting across from me, whom I had thought earlier was a nun, then stood up, stared directly at me, and announced, "God sent you."

5

TO THE CAMPAIGN

Here I was, in the new year of 1999, leading the charge to abolish the death penalty in Kentucky. The polls showed 70 percent of our citizens were dead set to keep it.

I did not have a publisher for my finished book. Pat read the manuscript, and he thought the book could be used in the campaign. We agreed to raise the money and the Kentucky Coalition to Abolish the Death Penalty would be the publisher.

Bill Butler was the man in Louisville who knew the most about publishing and printing, and he took an interest. Bill helped with the final editing and set the manuscript on a disc for printing. I had not yet decided on a title, and while we were discussing this I told Bill of the Chinese proverb, "The man who seeks revenge digs two graves." He suggested, *The Second Grave*, and that was it.

An artist friend of mine, Joe Fitzpatrick, designed the cover, and Bill Butler contracted with a Michigan printer for a thousand copies. It would take about ninety days to complete the printing. We sent her off.

In the early spring we hired Kaye Gallagher as our campaign coordinator. Pat found us an office in the Catholic Charities building in south Louisville near Churchill Downs, and we started.

Kaye was from a small town in southwestern Kentucky. She went to Western Kentucky University and decided she wanted to be a newspaper reporter. She got a job with the paper in Henderson, a town on the Ohio River, and there she met her husband to be, a young lawyer clerking for a federal judge. Kaye got to Louisville when her new husband accepted an offer from a law firm here. She was recommended to us by the preacher at her church, who, as it turned out, was the leader of the gay community in Henderson.

Kaye was one of the least judgmental people I've ever known. She decided whether she liked you as a person, and beyond that I don't believe there were any tests. Over time we became close friends.

Kaye, Pat, and I got organized with a computer and furniture for the office, all on loan, and our first stationery. Our office was in the same building as Pat's office so he was readily available. We worked around his schedule, met frequently, and made our plans.

We took the basic theme of the campaign from my book, and boiled the issues down to these points:

The Death Penalty is Unjust.

Too many mistakes are made. Repeatedly, cases come to light of inmates on death row who were wrongfully convicted. It is often the poor and minorities who are sentenced to death. Innocent people have been executed in other states. We can't let that happen in Kentucky.

The Death Penalty is Unnecessary.

Kentucky law included a sentence of life imprisonment without probation or parole in capital cases. If a defendant is found guilty of murder and is a continuing threat to society, incarceration for life provided justice for victims' families and protection for society. If it is later discovered a defendant has been wrongfully convicted, he is alive to be exonerated.

The Death Penalty is Expensive.

Studies of the economics of capital cases in Kentucky and other states conclude it costs at least $1 million more to prosecute a death penalty case than a life-without-parole case, including lifetime incarceration.

The Death Penalty is Not Effective.

Studies clearly show the death penalty does not deter murder. In fact highly publicized state killings have a brutalizing effect that breeds more violence in society.

We printed pamphlets with these points and with information about the coalition, and how to join KCADP. Now we needed to make a public announcement about the campaign. Pat suggested he schedule a KCADP membership meeting for June in Lexington and conclude it with a press conference on the Abolition Campaign and the publication of *The Second Grave*.

We agreed, so Kaye and all of us got busy planning the meeting and getting the word out to our members. We were rudely interrupted.

Eddie Lee Harper, an inmate on death row, sent word to his court appointed attorneys that he no longer wanted their assistance. He was withdrawing his pending appeals, and asked to be executed. He had had enough of death row!

Eddie Lee Harper had been convicted of killing Alice and Edward Harper, his adoptive mother and father. There was no doubt about his guilt. Harper had said he wanted to give up once before, but then changed his mind.

His attorneys resisted his decision to dismiss them and be executed on the grounds that he lacked the mental capacity to make this decision. They lost that final battle and Eddie Lee Harper got his wish to end his seventeen years on death row. The execution date was set for May 25 at 7:00 p.m.

As the new director of the Abolition Campaign I answered reporters' questions with a statement that I did not believe the Commonwealth of Kentucky should be an accomplice to a suicide.

Eddie Lee Harper spent his last day with his son and his grandchild and then was led to the execution chamber. He was not electrocuted as Harold McQueen had been. After we raised the issue of cruelty in the electrocution of Harold McQueen the Kentucky legislature enacted legislation adding lethal injection as an elective method of execution. That is what Eddie Lee Harper chose.

The new procedure was to inject sodium pentothal to cause unconsciousness; then pancuronium bromide to paralyze the lungs; and finally potassium chloride to stop the heart.

The protocol called for administering Valium ninety minutes before the execution to guard against the condemned person going into shock, making his veins inaccessible to the IV needle. The warden ordered this not be done so Eddie Lee Harper could be clearheaded enough to change his mind if he so chose.

He did not change his mind and at 7:28 p.m. he was pronounced dead.

Looking at the pictures of the equipment and reading the stories in the paper, the weird thing was how different this execution was. The electric chair execution looked like some medieval nightmare; the lethal injection procedure looked like a hospital operating room, the patient not surviving.

The Eddie Lee Harper case received an enormous amount of press, radio, and TV coverage. This was not the usual case of a condemned man fighting for his life and prosecutors and victims' families demanding justice. The news was a man seeking death by the state. This unusual twist made many people uncomfortable and the coverage brought attention to our Abolition Campaign and our upcoming annual meeting and press conference.

We received the shipment of a thousand copies of *The Second Grave* from the printer the day before Eddie Lee Harper was executed. When I had time to look at them and realize it was done, and there they were, I was a little overwhelmed, and pleased.

On June 5 we held the annual meeting of KCADP at the downtown Lexington Public Library and had a great turnout. After the meeting we held our press conference on the steps of the library and had good media coverage.

We announced the Abolition Campaign, the publication

of *The Second Grave*, said wise things, and we thought it all came off very well. Then the high excitement was over, the campaign was under way, and it was time for the nitty-gritty work.

Scott Wegenast, one of the principals at the Catholic Conference in Frankfort, had experience with web sites and with his help we soon had www.kcadp.org up and running. Pat learned the essentials and he kept the site current and interesting.

I sat down and wrote a twenty-minute speech, first explaining why I was involved and then making the four basic points in our argument. Kaye and I then organized a speakers' bureau. Within a few months we had twelve volunteer participants who studied the pertinent facts and the points to be made, and then each prepared his or her own speech about the issues and why they were involved. We practiced our speeches within the group and they all turned out pretty well.

Kaye sent letters to every Kiwanis, Optimist, Rotary, Elk, Chamber of Commerce, and other civic organizations she could find. She made follow-up telephone calls, and gradually speaking opportunities around the state surfaced. I think this was a struggle for many chairs of entertainment committees. Most of them didn't want to have a controversial program, certainly not about the death penalty, but they did need to fill the speakers' slot for every meeting – so frequently they decided to take a chance on us. Many of these meetings were a real hoot.

My very first one was for a civic group meeting at a Holiday Inn off the Outer Loop south of Louisville. I have made many speeches in my life and tried jury cases, and beforehand I always have butterflies in my stomach. On this occasion you would have thought I was arguing before the Supreme Court of the United States.

I found the Holiday Inn, and found the meeting room (Parlor B), and walked in to find three people sitting at a table fiddling with their coffee cups. One of them looked up and said, "You the speaker?" I was tempted to lie and beat a retreat but I didn't.

Eventually the room filled to a total of six people, four men and two women. They did their ceremonial things, made several comments about how no one much came to the meeting anymore and then the chairman introduced me, reading a short typed paragraph I had given him.

I've seen a lack of enthusiasm in my fellow men on more than one occasion, but this one had to be the ultimate. Not only did the four men fold their arms across their chests and lower their chins as they half listened, they occasionally gave deep sighs and rolled their eyes. I gave them facts. I gave them opinions, and I concluded as gracefully as I could. There was light applause.

The chair, without getting up from his slouched seating position, said, "Next month we're going to have Joe Little tell us about the drainage problems at the Babe Ruth baseball diamond. We certainly thank today's speaker for being here, and the meeting is adjourned."

I put my notes away, gathered my box of campaign materials, and after nodding to the chairman headed for the door. One of the two women present angled across the room and intercepted me just at the exit. She leaned close and spoke softly in my ear so the others wouldn't hear, "I think you're right, and I believe Thelma (nodding toward the other lady) does too. May I buy a copy of your book? How much is it?"

My mood, my life, my future and that of mankind, was transformed. "Ten dollars," I replied as I made my first "after the speech" sale. When I left the Holiday Inn and got back on the expressway, I drove with the light heart and ready smile of a man who had just remade the world.

We had two book signings in Louisville and Lexington bookstores during the summer, got some good reviews in the papers, and sold some copies. I was sensitive about my book. When I heard compliments, I was embarrassed. If the book were slighted in any way, I was offended. I got over it.

I received a call one day from the producer of the Sue Wylie Talk Show asking if I would come on her radio show. I knew she was on a Lexington station and was popular, but I had never listened to it, so I asked Pat what he thought.

"Absolutely," he said. "The experience will do you a world of good." By his laugh I could tell I was in trouble, but what the hell.

Sue Wylie was a very personable woman and accommodated me by setting up my participation by telephone from my home in Louisville. This made it quite easy, and on the appointed day I was ready to go.

Once we were on the air, Sue Wylie struck without mercy. She asked me, "You think we should coddle these guys who kill and rape and beat people without mercy? You want to keep them in fancy jails, like motels, with TVs and computers and exercise rooms? Personally mister, they're not fit to live, certainly not on my tax dollars," and on she went.

I got in my arguments and facts as best I could when I could, but it was pretty hopeless.

Then she got to the calls, and some of the people who called in made her sound like a sweetheart. I soon realized the only possible goal here was survival.

One caller, who sounded like an old geezer, quoted Old Testament scripture to me about killing for the Lord, and asked me how I could preach against the Bible. I replied that God had spared Cain at the very first murder, and marked him so no one would do him harm. That was my example from the Bible.

The old man on the line, in high dudgeon, shot back, "but that was 'fore de flood."

"Alright," I replied, not knowing really what he meant.

After the program, when I recovered from the pummeling, I looked up Noah and the flood and found out about the Noachian Code, and by golly the old geezer was right, and I learned something.

• • • •

We sent a gift copy of *The Second Grave* with a cover letter about the campaign to every legislator, and we set up appointments to talk personally to any of them who would see us.

We arranged to meet with officials in Governor Paul Patton's office. We selected individuals whom we thought might be receptive to our mission, told them about the campaign, gave them a copy of *The Second Grave*. We learned what we could about the politics of the coming session and the governor's take on things.

Governor Patton had been a coal mine operator in Eastern Kentucky and made a fortune in the coal boom of the 1970s. When he decided to get into politics he was elected Pike County Judge Executive, and then ended up as our governor. He was a bright and energetic man who wanted to do well leading the state and the Democratic Party. His goals included improving education in Kentucky, particularly higher education, and conserving Kentucky's natural beauty.

We understood the governor was for the death penalty, but we were uncertain how strong an issue it was with him. When we were with people in his administration we listened hard to get a feeling for what he might do. For instance, if we got an abolition bill passed, would he sign it?

In the course of our prodding and listening one official said to me:

"You understand the governor and his wife are from Eastern Kentucky, and that can be a different world. There is violence in most every family history in Eastern Kentucky, and the governor and his wife, Judy, are no exception. When Judy Patton was a child, her father was the county sheriff. He was shot dead, on their front porch I believe, right on the spot. And that's not the end of it. Judy Patton's first husband was murdered. They may not look at killing the same as you and I do."

I suspected that had to be true. My own feelings about killing, and preventing killings, were conflicted. On one hand I was an eternal optimist about the world and its people and how things would turn out, and at the same time I was aware of the dark side of man's nature. We were, I thought, all in the same boat, laughing and crying, and rocking it perilously.

Summer came. Kaye, Pat and I continued our odyssey throughout Kentucky, wherever they would have us. We spoke and peddled the book and handed out pamphlets urging abolition. Our audiences, no matter how incredulous they were, no matter how crazy wrong they thought us to be, were invariably polite. Sometimes their politeness bordered on condescension, but they were never rude.

The insufferably hot days of August and September came and slowly passed and the small yellow leaves of the birches began to fall, and the oak and maples began to turn. Fall comes to Kentucky with leisurely steps, moving slowly to glorious days of color and cool breezes, transcending into the folds of wintertime.

It occurred to me, thanks to these civic club appearances, that I have probably recited the Pledge of Allegiance before, and sung Happy Birthday to, more strangers than most anyone you will ever know.

Mensa asked me to speak at their monthly dinner meeting and there were about twenty to twenty-five in attendance. Mensa members have great IQ test scores. I easily remember their president's name: Joe McCarthy. The conversation at dinner was, believe me, not like at a Kiwanis or Rotary gathering. These people were really interested in themselves and how intelligent they were and they wanted me to know and understand this. Joe McCarthy was himself an insurance adjuster.

One of the things they discussed was what a fine organization they had, how difficult it was to get in, and how proud they all were to be members. To make conversation I asked what the local Mensa group did. A lady at my table responded. "You know," she said, "we had a retreat a couple of years ago to discuss that very thing—our mission and what good things we might do. You know, after we talked it through what we decided?"

Of course I did not know and I nodded in the negative.

"We decided," she said, and then paused dramatically, "We decided to do nothing." All in all, it was my best judgment they made a wise decision.

One week we were invited to speak to the Rotary Luncheon in Hopkinsville, in far Western Kentucky. This region is called the Jackson Purchase because its purchase was negotiated with the Indians by Andrew Jackson.

The land is flat and low as it makes its way to the Mississippi river. The soil is suited for tobacco and lies over thick veins of high sulphur coal that is stripped from the land by scrapers the size of large buildings.

It was a long drive from Louisville and Kaye and I took turns driving. We talked sometimes and were quiet for long periods. At one time I asked her if she knew about the Black Patch War.

"Only a little bit," she replied, "did you write about it in your book? Tell me about it?"

"It all began," I said, and told her the story.

The Black Patch War was one of a number of economic wars in America in the late 1800s. The Duke Trust, led by "Buck" Duke, son of the founder of the American Tobacco Company, gained a monopoly in the dark chewing tobacco market. He used that control to force the auction price of dark tobacco below the costs of the Western Kentucky tobacco growers. Farmers went broke, banks foreclosed, and in desperation the tobacco growers organized to fight back. A secret militia was formed to break the Duke monopoly, and ultimately the tobacco farmers prevailed.

Robert Penn Warren's first novel, *The Night Riders*, was about the violence of the Black Patch War, and the effect it had on many good souls.

Kaye listened to every word and the story's end found us near Hopkinsville and our friends at the Rotary. The meeting was held in what looked like a very new "Memorial Building" downtown. The meeting room was exceptionally large, with a series of equally spaced cloth-covered tables marching up and down the great expanse. I thought as I looked that this scene could be a mystic ceremony any time back through the millennia.

When lunch was finished the meeting began and the first person recognized to speak was the attorney who was responsible for getting us our invitation. He said, without further explanation, "The subject for the talk today is the death penalty. Wouldn't it be more appropriate if we had this talk at Easter rather than at Christmastime?"

No one knew quite where to look, and there was no response. Finally the chairwoman rose and said, "I'll now call on the Reverend (somebody, I don't remember his name) to say a few words at this time."

The good reverend was a local Baptist preacher and his mission was to give a eulogy for a departed member who was known as "Dipper." He was quite animated about the lost Dipper and how we all missed him. As he looked around at his audience the preacher suddenly stopped mid-sentence as he noticed for the first time the room decorations. His eyes were saucers as he wailed, "What am I—a Baptist preacher—doing in these surroundings?"

The walls of our room were decorated from floor to ceiling with stacked empty cases of Budweiser beer. There was an unending recitation circling the entire room, "Bud Light." Cases were stacked on the stage behind the podium where he spoke. We were surrounded by bright red beer cases placed with elaborate care and effort for a reception to be hosted by the local beer distributor that evening.

The laughter and cracks that accompanied the Baptist minister's distress went off in various directions and the death of Dipper was forgotten.

When it was my turn I made my usual speech and put in some local references to the Black Patch War and the invasion of Hopkinsville. One of the points that I stressed was that the death penalty was not a deterrent to murder. I cited statistics that showed the murder rate was higher in death penalty states than it was in the twelve states that no longer had the death penalty. The best I could tell, all those raised faces were taking this in pretty well and later when I asked for questions a hand came up from an old skinny guy in the back on my left.

I pointed to him and he raised himself slowly from his chair and said, "I heard what you said that executions don't stop murders and that reminds me of something that happened back home. I'm not from around here," he said looking around, "I was born and raised in the mountains in Eastern Kentucky. One time back home they were getting ready to hang this man for murder and rape and before they released that trap they asked him if he had anything he wanted to say. This man looked at them and said, "Well, there's one thing I want you to know, I sure learned my lesson."

• • • •

The very best public event we had in the campaign was one that I had very little to do with. Here is how it happened.

I encouraged young people to get involved in the campaign and back in the spring we had a meeting with several young activists in Louisville who expressed an interest in abolition. We asked them what they wanted to do in the campaign. It may come as no surprise that they decided they wanted an event. A Youth Against Violence rally. Well, why not. I said, "Okay, but it's your show. You have to organize it, and you have to do it. We will give you support and expense money (I promised $1,000), but the blood, sweat, and tears of making it happen has to be yours."

They preferred it that way. They soon had a working group of young people from Louisville and Lexington that organized and held a Youth Against Violence rally on a fall Saturday afternoon on the capitol lawn in Frankfort. It was as wonderful an event as I have ever attended.

With Pat's help they got a commitment from Steve Earle, the singer/composer who did music for the movie, *Dead Man Walking*, and who had done time himself. I had never heard of

Steve Earle, but all of the kids had, and he helped attract a hell of a crowd. They also had three local rock bands and three speakers.

This Saturday afternoon was as only a fall afternoon can be in Kentucky. It was perfect. The air was still warm, the sun was bright, but there was the smell and feel of fall mixed with the background of yellow and red maples and oaks. It was the kind of day you just want to take a deep breath, close your eyes, lean your head back, and say, "Thanks!"

Some of the group made white cutouts, shaped like the head and shoulders of a person, and stood them in close formation on one section of the lawn. They numbered the same as the number of executions in Kentucky. From a distance they looked like markers in a military cemetery. Photographers and TV cameramen had a field day.

Almost four hundred young people from all over the state came and participated. There were picnics on the lawn and tables where our pamphlets were distributed and my book was sold. Some of our coalition partners, such as the ACLU, had their own tables and literature.

The rock bands played, young people spoke their message, and even though late, Steve Earle showed (of course, for free) and played while the kids listened and hooted and swayed back and forth.

When Steve Earle sang his last song, and the last short speech was given, everyone up and down the lawn stood and recited a "Pledge Against Violence" that the young people composed. I looked about and listened to their earnest voices and watched their faces, and I thanked my lucky stars that this was where I was and these were the people I was with on this glorious Saturday afternoon in Kentucky.

6

GETTING READY

I decided, because of my lack of experience as a lobbyist, to place a priority on personally meeting with legislators before the legislative session; and with those meetings, hopefully, I could better plan our legislative strategy. Politics are never easy, and it is said politics are the damnedest in Kentucky. A little history may help.

Most of what is now Kentucky was the western part of Virginia until 1792, when the new state was formed. Our lands were separated from Virginia by the Appalachian Mountains. In the early days it took enormous energy and stamina and luck to make it across those mountains and survive the risks of the wilderness and the Indians.

Following the Revolutionary War the numbers of people seeking adventure and a better life on the western lands increased exponentially, and hundreds of thousands of hunters, trappers, land speculators, and settlers climbed through the Cumberland Gap from Virginia and moved on into Kentucky and Missouri. Another route was down the Ohio River from Pennsylvania, along the northern border of Kentucky to settlements like Louisville, or on to the Mississippi and St. Louis.

As the numbers grew the idea of self-government grew. Many of the new settlers thought seriously about establishing a separate country, but those preferring statehood prevailed. After ten constitutional conventions a state charter was agreed upon, the Kentucky-Virginia Compact was signed, and Kentucky became the fifteenth state in the Union.

There was a serious civic tug of war for the location of the capitol of the new state. The rapidly growing river town of Louisville was so intent on becoming the capitol city it built a capitol to house the legislature right in the middle of town. The city of Lexington in the heart of the Bluegrass Country with close ties to the Eastern Kentucky settlers and the Central Kentucky tobacco farmers also wished to have the capitol, and lobbied the issue strenuously.

But the small town of Frankfort, in a pleasant valley of the Kentucky River, about halfway between the two combatants, was selected as the site of the capitol. It is a beautiful site.

The western approach is along a ridge of hills looking down on the town lying close on both sides of the river. The marble edifice of the capitol's dome reaches up to the hills and to the Kentucky sky. It is stately, and there are almost no visible parts that are not marble.

The legislature had one nundred representatives elected for two-year terms, and thirty-eight senators with four-year terms. The legislature met at the capitol for sixty days in even numbered years. The legislature had been controlled by conservative Democrats since the Civil War, although occasionally a Republican had slipped in as governor.

But times were changing, and as the state became ever more conservative the Republicans gained seats, particularly in the Senate. Just recently two Democratic senators were persuaded to change their party affiliation to Republican. Their votes gave the Kentucky Republicans control of the Senate for the first time since the Civil War. The Democrats were flabbergasted when it happened, and then furious at their impotence to prevent it.

Our initial strategy was to concentrate our efforts in the House of Representatives, where we thought we had considerably more strength than in the Senate. We identified key Democratic leaders in the House and members of the Judiciary Committee, and set out to meet with as many of them as possible before the session began.

The Judiciary Committee was one of sixteen standing House committees. Its jurisdiction included legal matters, judges, the courts, and the criminal justice system. Any bill affecting the death penalty went to the Judiciary Committee. The committee had seventeen members, including the chair, and because the House was heavily Democratic, eleven members were Democrats and six Republicans.

The rules of the House of Representatives provided, "The committee chairman, or the committee by majority vote in a regularly called meeting, shall post...the bills and resolutions to be considered at its next meeting..." Thus, the chair of the committee could control its docket.

When we lobbied for the Racial Justice Act, Mike Bowling was chair of Judiciary. He retired and Representative Gross Lindsay was appointed by the Democratic leadership to replace him. They were two quite different men.

Representative Lindsay lived in the small river town of Henderson in Western Kentucky, and lo and behold, Henderson's Lions International invited me to be its speaker at a luncheon meeting in October. Kaye got us an appointment with Gross Lindsay in the early afternoon following my speech. We were off to Henderson.

My speech at the Lions meeting went fine. They gave me a coffee mug with the Lions International insignia, and then Kaye and I headed for the office of the chair of the Judiciary Committee.

Gross Lindsay is a longtime lawyer with a one-man office. We were shown into his cluttered office and he rose to greet us amiably, and seemed genuinely surprised we had gone to the trouble to come visit. He is a short, squat man, and what little hair he has above his ears is clipped short and we couldn't tell he had any at all. His head sat large on his shoulders without benefit of a neck and he looked over half glasses which sat at the end of a bumpy nose. His smile had a one-sided twist to it, which, for some reason, made me wonder if we were laughing at the same thing.

After a few amenities Kaye and I told Representative Lindsay about KCADP and the reasons we opposed the death penalty. He leaned back in a swivel chair behind his desk; his eyes became smaller as he wrinkled up his nose and squinted at us. I finished our presentation and told him briefly about writing *The Second* Grave. Kaye asked him if he had received his copy in the mail. He shrugged and looked nonplussed and Kaye gave him a copy, told him it was a gift with our compliments.

When we finished he put the book aside, leaned forward on his desk, and said, "Most people think executions are necessary, and I don't think you're likely to change it." His tone was matter of fact, and his face was sour.

One of the arguments I used on the subject of changing public attitudes and opinions was that Kentucky had achieved a complete constitutional overhaul of its judicial system about ten years ago. In more recent times the legislature had revamped our public education system in a plan called KERA. KERA was beginning to work well and was being used as a model in other states. Both these efforts took a lot of doing, and many pundits were surprised they were successful.

I gently brought forth those thoughts to Representative Lindsay to illustrate abolition of the death penalty was possible inasmuch as Kentucky had reformed its court system and its public school system.

I hit a nerve. Representative Lindsay's large head, which had been quite pallid, was now a rose red as he responded, "KERA is an abomination. That was one of the damn most foolish things the Kentucky legislature ever did. Let me tell you, my wife is a school teacher, has been for forty years, and I know, and my wife will tell you, KERA is one of the worst things ever done to the teachers of Kentucky, and the students."

Well, we listened for some time and it was clear the KERA reforms to Kentucky's school system were not supported by Mrs. Lindsay, or her husband, and there was no way I could think of to change the subject.

I don't know how we weathered the storm but we did sit there until it abated, and then Representative Lindsay said, "I've got things to do," and we thanked him for his time and we left.

As we walked down the main street of this small town Kaye looked at me and said, "Now we know." It obviously wasn't good, but I wasn't too sure what all I really did know about Representative Lindsay.

I knew he was getting old and grumpy, and his wife wasn't happy with school reform, but this man was chair of the Judiciary Committee and had a lot of power. How had that come about? As events unfolded I found out a lot about Gross Lindsay, as we will see.

We continued our mission undeterred, with speeches and meetings and events. I participated in a debate at Centre College but it wasn't much of a contest. The assistant commonwealth attorney speaking in favor of the death penalty recited Kentucky statutes outlining what the commonwealth attorney did. The young audience was impatient with him and mostly on my side anyway. I think he was glad to get out of there.

Pat and I met with the editorial board of the Lexington *Herald Leader*, and we both thought that went well. One of their members was outspoken against us, but we appeared to have the majority of the editorial board. The *Herald Leader* had not taken a position on the death penalty so we hoped that at the right time they would support us.

We also met with the Jefferson County delegation - all the legislators, Republicans and Democrats, from the Louisville area. They listened to our presentation about our hopes and plans for the coming session without making any comment. Their members covered a wide political spectrum and we anticipated strong support from some of them.

One of the most encouraging sessions we had that fall was with the vice-chair of the Judiciary Committee, Rob Wilkey. I went to see him at his office and found him a most personable man with a neatly trimmed beard, much younger than Gross

Lindsay. Rob Wilkey was a lawyer and lived and worked in Scottsville, in south-central Kentucky.

I had no sooner outlined why I was there, when Rob Wilkey took over. He talked for almost fifteen minutes and basically made all the points I cover in my Rotary speech. He knew all our arguments and professed to being completely convinced, and on our side.

I felt like I'd died and gone to heaven, and then I turned the subject to the Judiciary Committee and Wilkey's role as vice-chair. Representative Wilkey's effusiveness faded and he became much more cautious discussing the committee and its chair. I asked him as directly as I thought I could if he would sponsor a death penalty abolition bill in the Judiciary Committee. He somberly replied that he'd think about it and perhaps talk to the chairman about it, but it was too early to make any specific commitments. My impression as I left our long and friendly meeting was that Representative Wilkey was a very nice guy who, while he was against the death penalty, wanted very much to be liked and to get along with everyone, particularly with the chair of the Judiciary Committee.

When I researched statistics on abolishing the death penalty I found sixty percent of those supporting abolition were women. I liked those odds, so we made a special effort with the women in the Kentucky legislature. One was Senator Elizabeth Tori of Radcliff.

Senator Tori represented a rural area that was becoming increasingly urbanized. She worked in the real estate business and she was doing well. She graciously gave me an appointment and off I trotted in search of what I hoped was a natural ally.

I entered her office and we made pleasantries as I found a seat opposite her. I hadn't met her, and as I looked at her for the first time I realized this was no ordinary woman. I'm not good at ages and I was guessing at mid-fifties. (A later check showed I was low by a decade.) She was thin and tan. She wore a short light colored skirt, which appeared shorter when she was sitting down, and over a light blouse she had on a jacket with imitation fur on the lapels and cuffs. This was considerable to take in.

I got myself on task and told her about the campaign, our coalition members, the many churches, and the basic reasons we were campaigning to end the death penalty.

She appeared to be listening, with a small smile of interest on her face. It occurred to me as I got more used to the surroundings that probably this lady had been through a lot. No doubt it had taken considerable scheming and hard work for her to become a state senator.

I moved the subject to the abolition of the death penalty for juveniles and called her special attention to a proposed bill which raised the death penalty eligibility age from sixteen to eighteen. I talked about the late emotional and cognitive development of children which often extends into their early twenties. She looked at me with greater interest. When I paused as I was getting ready to conclude, she said, "You know what?" I continued my pause, and thought rather than muttered, "What?"

"We own some real estate, some buildings, and do you know what those kids of yours do?" My pause continued, now with apprehension.

"Those kids put stuff all over the sides of my buildings. Not just once, but a bunch of times…graffiti…all sorts of stuff…some of it about me.

"You know what I'd like to do to those kids?"

She was on a roll, and I was getting ready to duck.

"What we should do to those kids is a caning…a public caning, downtown. That would be the last time they'd paint on my buildings, I tell you."

Senator Tori was not kidding, and if there was another way to take the conversation I was neither smart nor brave enough to pull it off. In just a little bit I thanked her for her time and headed back to my own territory. I wondered if there was some way I could find out what was in the graffiti about Senator Tori.

These exploratory meetings showed very practical

problems we faced trying to change a centuries old culture and system. I had a discussion about this one day with Rowly Brucken, the head of Amnesty International in Kentucky, one of our coalition partners.

Rowly was working on his Ph.D in political science at Ohio State and lived in Kentucky because his wife was a Presbyterian minister here. One of his major academic interests was the history of social movements in the United States. He told me:

"If you look at successful campaigns to bring on major changes in social behavior you will invariably find that the first requirement is a well organized, long-range, well-financed campaign of dedicated hard-working people. This we are achieving. But the second and all-important requirement is an unexpected event, which for whatever reason throws the social gyroscope off center enough that change is possible.

"What is needed to make any major social change possible is an intervention—a miracle!

"The Civil Rights movement of the late fifties and early sixties was well organized but was going nowhere in terms of legislation until the country was turned upside down by Kennedy's assassination. Johnson recognized the moment, and used it to pass the Civil Rights Act of 1964.

"The social ramifications of World War I made the Nineteenth Amendment possible in 1920 after a hundred years of campaigning. What a social movement needs is blood, sweat, and tears, and then an intervention."

That struck me with a ring of practical truth. In a campaign to abolish the death penalty, what would that intervention, that unexpected miracle, be?

One answer was obvious. The ultimate fear of death penalty advocates was executing an innocent man. We needed a man on death row to be found innocent. Since life is stranger than fiction, I thought we found one. Here is how it happened.

Late in October, Father Richard Sullivan, pastor of St.

James Catholic Parish in Elizabethtown invited me, Pat, and Kaye to a small gathering of some of his parishioners whom he hoped would give money to the Abolition Campaign.

I talked to the gathered parishioners about my book and the campaign; Pat and Kaye spoke of our needs and the reasons abolition was right. We raised over three thousand dollars that night. Right before we left Father Sullivan asked, "Have you heard about Frank Tamme's case?" I shook my head no. I remembered from reviewing the cases of the men on death row that Tamme had been convicted of a double murder, was about at the end of his appeals string, and was soon to be up for execution.

"You may be interested in Frank's case. If you've got time stay a minute and I'll tell you."

The parishioners had gone so Kaye, Pat, and I stopped, sat down again and looked at Father Sullivan.

In a remake of "Boy's Town" Dick Sullivan would be the priest. He was handsome and dark haired, with the most gentle and loving expression imaginable. He was a man of his convictions and firmly went about his mission. When things didn't go right, he often would say, with a soft smile, tilting his head to one side, "Well, that's the way it is sometimes."

He looked at us now quite seriously, although his face was seldom far from a smile.

"You probably don't know this, but Frank Tamme and I grew up together in Boyle County. We went to the same school, St. Peter and Paul parochial school in Danville, and since there were just a few of us boys, we played all the sports together.

"Frank and I were good buddies, but in high school we started going with different crowds and didn't see as much of each other. He got into some sort of trouble with the law in his senior year, and apparently one of the options the Judge gave him was to go into the army, so he went to Vietnam. I think he had at least a year of combat there.

"Well, after that I lost track, and of course now a lot of years have passed, although occasionally my family back home would say something about the Tamme family and what Frank was doing.

"Long after he got into all this murder trouble I got a call from his lawyer asking if I would come to a hearing on Frank's sentence and be a character witness, and I said I would.

"Honestly, to the extent I ever thought about it, I assumed since a judge and a jury had found Frank guilty, that he had done it. It was tough for me to imagine because Frank was hardly the killer type, but you know, if you go through the trial and all, you assume the guy is guilty.

"I went to the hearing and after I talked to the lawyer I got to see Frank in his jail cell. I mean to tell you that was tough. I hadn't seen him in years, and of course we both had changed, but I mean, he had really changed. He looked so much older.

"We talked about family and stuff and then I said, 'Frank, how can I help you?'

"He looked at me. And, of course, no matter how much people change, if you knew them as a kid you still think of them and see them as a kid. And Frank is looking right at me, and he says, 'Dick, I know all this looks terrible, but I tell you, and it's the God's honest truth, I swear I did not kill those two guys.

"'I did do some dumb stuff. We were all into growing marijuana and selling some coke, and I knew those two guys, but I didn't kill them.'"

Dick Sullivan took a deep breath and said, "I don't know if I'm right or not, but I believed him. And I believe him now.

"I didn't do him much good at the hearing because all I could say was I knew him and his family when I was a kid. But I hadn't seen him for a long time and didn't know anything about what he was doing at the time of the murders. So, he still is set to be executed. But I did call the agency in Frankfort that's defending him, what's it called?"

"The D.P.A., Department of Public Advocacy," Pat filled in.

"Yes, the D.P.A., and I told them about my meeting with Frank and that I thought maybe he was innocent, and I asked them how could I help. And they told me, money. If they had money they could hire an investigator to check out some of the facts about the murder that they thought could make a difference.

"I asked them how much money and they told me five thousand dollars. You probably don't know this, but my mother died last year and I inherited her small estate. I sent them a check for five thousand dollars from the estate."

Dick Sullivan said this so simply and unaffectedly that it sounded as if he were telling us he had made a phone call or written a letter.

"Well," he continued, "D.P.A. hired an investigator, and she investigated the whole case.

"I know this is getting long, but that's not all.

"There is a lawyer, Kenyon Meyer, who was in my parish when I was in Louisville. He and his fiancée came to me about this same time and asked if I'd marry them. During the course of planning the wedding Kenyon heard me mention Tamme's case and the death penalty and he said that he thought he should get involved in some pro bono death penalty cases. I encouraged him to volunteer and well, he did, and they assigned him Frank Tamme's case. He's done a lot of work on it, and I know about it in bits and pieces, but you should really get updated by him."

The three of us looked at each other. Was Frank Tamme our innocent man on death row? When I got home Sunday night I dug into the papers I had on Frank Tamme and it wasn't much, so Monday morning I called Kenyon Meyer.

I didn't know Kenyon Meyer but he was very pleasant on the telephone and when I told him I was interested in Frank Tamme he suggested I come down to his office and talk. He was available for a few minutes that morning. I went immediately and after a brief conversation he brought all the documents in Frank Tamme's case into the conference room. I went to work, and this is the story as I pieced it out.

When Frank Tamme returned from Vietnam at age twenty-one he was a different man. He had seen a year of combat and a lot of drugs, and he had lost a lot of time. After he was discharged he went home and attended nearby Alice Lloyd College. After graduation he got a job at the Kentucky State Employment Office in Danville. There wasn't much in the files about his personal life, but he did get married, had a family, and there was a note that his son had been killed in a motorcycle accident.

One of the major cash crops in southeastern Kentucky was marijuana, and the Tamme family farm was an ideal out of the way location for a marijuana patch. Frank Tamme knew about marijuana from his experiences in the army in Vietnam, and before long he was growing and selling it. The money was good.

As business grew he leased some land on a couple of other farms nearby and the operation got so big he had to bring other men in to help. Three of these men were Bill Buchanan, Neal Maddox, and Harold Southerland.

Neal Maddox and Harold Southerland disappeared on August 11, 1983. They were last seen near Danville. Two weeks later Harold Southerland's car was found in a dump at Scott's Ridge. Detectives searching the car found an old telephone bill that listed all the numbers he had called, and one of them was Tamme's. The detectives went to see Frank Tamme and questioned him about the two missing men. Tamme told them he knew nothing about their disappearance. The detectives had no evidence he did, and the murders remained unsolved.

Over a year later, on September 22, 1984, Bill Buchanan was at his farm and the story is that two masked men appeared, tied him up, and stole a thousand of his marijuana plants. Buchanan believed Frank Tamme was one of the masked men.

Two days later Bill Buchanan went to the Kentucky State Police and told them he knew where the two missing men, Neal Maddox and Harold Southerland, were buried and who had killed them. He took the police to a remote site in Washington County where they discovered the remains of two bodies. Bill Buchanan told the police he had watched Frank Tamme kill the two men, burn their bodies, and bury them over a year ago.

The bodies were identified, and based on the testimony of Bill Buchanan the Washington County Grand Jury indicted Frank Tamme and Bill Buchanan for the murder of Neal Maddox and Harold Southerland.

Bill Buchanan's lawyer asked the court to separate the trial of the two defendants, and the court granted the motion. Tamme's trial was scheduled first. Frank Tamme had a family and some money, and he was able to pay for one of Danville's best defense attorneys to represent him.

The prosecution's case against Frank Tamme was based almost entirely on the testimony of Bill Buchanan. There was no physical evidence implicating Tamme and the defense attorney thought Tamme was being framed by Buchanan and that the case was weak. Frank Tamme and his family had no extra money for an independent investigation of the case, so there wasn't any.

At the trial Bill Buchanan testified Frank Tamme had murdered the two men and the prosecution put forth the theory that a love triangle produced the motive. Harold Southerland was separated from his wife and she was reputedly having an affair with Frank Tamme.

Defense counsel put on no witnesses and thought he could win the case on the lack of substantive proof against his client. There was a problem at the trial however. Over the defense's objection the prosecutor was permitted to introduce testimony that Frank Tamme was a major drug dealer in the area.

When it was over, the jury found Frank Tamme guilty of double murder, and he was sentenced to be executed.

Frank Tamme was out of money, and his local defense attorney was replaced with lawyers from the Department of Public Advocacy's Post Conviction section. These attorneys did a lot of capital appeal cases and they decided in Tamme's case to concentrate their appeals on the grounds that there was little substantive evidence tying Tamme to the crime and that it was improper to inject the subject of drugs into the case.

All of this took a long time, but eventually the appeal got

to the Kentucky Supreme Court where, after briefs and oral arguments, the court handed down a decision reversing Tamme's conviction. The major problem that the court found was the introduction of the evidence of drug dealings by the prosecution.

The case came back to the circuit court for a retrial and a new date was set. Although the guilty verdict in the first trial had been a surprise, certainly to the defense, the case up to this point had been nothing out of the ordinary for a capital case. From this point on things got strange.

Frank Tamme did not get his retrial when it was first set, and there were delays until 1993. He was on death row all this time. The delays came from four different judges being on and off the case for different reasons. One died, one was opposed to the death penalty, and so on. The trial was further delayed because of changes in defense counsel. Appointed attorneys came and went as counsel for Frank Tamme.

When Frank Tamme's second trial finally began he was represented by two attorneys, a woman and a man, whom he liked and trusted. These two attorneys decided, with the strong encouragement of the prosecuting attorney, that the supreme court's decision setting aside Tamme's first conviction because the prosecution had introduced evidence about drug dealing, meant there could be no mention of drugs in the new trial—not only by the prosecution but also by the defense witnesses.

After the first trial and conviction, Frank Tamme got very active in the defense of his case. He told his lawyers that since he had not committed the murders, Bill Buchanan, the prosecutor's star witness, must be the one. There must have been some falling out between Buchanan and the two murdered men, some argument, probably over drug money. If this was the best explanation of what had happened and the best defense, it was necessary that Frank Tamme testify in his own defense and the fact that these four men worked together growing and selling marijuana had to be disclosed.

Frank Tamme's two lawyers shook their heads and said

they were sorry but the way they (and the prosecutor) interpreted the supreme court's opinion, no one could mention drugs.

This meant that Bill Buchanan could, and did, testify against Frank Tamme and Frank Tamme could not present his defense. He could not tell what had happened, as he knew it. It was then that Frank Tamme lost hope. The second trial ended and the jury came back with a verdict of guilty.

At the hearing following the trial to determine Frank Tamme's sentence Father Dick Sullivan was called to testify. At the conclusion of that hearing the jury recommended the death sentence for Frank Tamme, and the judge approved it.

As I was finishing putting these events all together, Kenyon Meyer came back to the conference room to see how I was doing.

"I'm at the point where Tamme was sentenced the second time and Father Dick Sullivan was involved, and I guess you were soon to come on the scene."

"Okay. First, you will not believe what happened to me in this case. I volunteered to help, for sure, but I mostly practice corporate law and what I understood when I took the case was that D.P.A. would send me all the records and I would have a couple of months to go through them and then get caught up on criminal law and figure out how I could help.

"That is not what happened. I no sooner received all these boxes of records – I hadn't even opened them—when we got notice that Frank's execution date had been set for April 9. I called D.P.A. and said, 'What is this? What am I supposed to do?' They said sometimes this happens; the attorney general is forcing the case. What do I do? They said I had to file motions for a stay of the execution – 'You've got thirty days.'

"My partner and I dropped everything we were doing and took on the case. We met with the experts with D.P.A., read the criminal law, and started drafting motions for a stay of execution. We got the papers filed in time and a stay was granted because Tamme's appeals had not been exhausted. Later we heard about the investigator that was hired with Father Sullivan's check. Her name was Diana Queen, and she said she was ready to make a report. Well, we went to see her and I am telling you this is getting exciting for us. This woman had done investigating work for years and she really knew what she was doing.

"She reported that she first concentrated on Bill Buchanan. She knew he had been indicted along with Frank Tamme. She went back through the court records to see if Bill Buchanan had ever been tried, or what had happened to the case against him, since he admitted in his testimony that he had witnessed the two murders.

"Diana Queen found out a lot about Bill Buchanan. He had been into drugs in a big way before and after the two murders. He had been caught in LaRue County by an undercover agent and had been indicted for possession and trafficking in drugs. He was out on bond when he went to the police and told them the Tamme story and took them to the two bodies. The police bought his story and asked him if he would testify in court against Frank Tamme.

"Bill Buchanan told them that he would testify, but that he had a problem. He would not testify if he were serving time on the drug charges in LaRue County. The prosecutor called the officials in LaRue. They made a deal that LaRue County wouldn't prosecute on the drug charges if Bill Buchanan testified against Tamme in the double murder case in Washington County.

"This agreement, Diana Queen told me, was never revealed to the defense during Tamme's two trials, and no jury ever knew what Bill Buchanan was getting in return for his testimony against Tamme.

"I told the investigator she had cracked the case wide open and she said she had more and better stuff.

"In the second trial, she told me, there was a witness for the defense who said he had heard Bill Buchanan admit that he had killed the two men. No one paid much attention to this at the trial because it was brought out that this witness was a felon and had committed perjury, and was just a guy trying to help Frank Tamme.

"When she checked in to this she found that this witness claimed Bill Buchanan had made this statement on a trip to Texas to buy marijuana, and that there was a third person on the trip. Diana Queen set out to find that third person to see what he would say, and she found him.

"The guy's name was Steve Armstrong. He was out of the state during Tamme's two trials, and didn't know about them. Diana Queen found him down south somewhere; he remembered the trip to Texas very well, and Diana Queen convinced him to drive back to Kentucky and testify.

"He testified that he used to work in construction around Danville but was injured in an accident and was laid off. When he and his family got hurting for money he thought maybe he could make some money in marijuana and not get caught. He was told he could make a quick $2,000 by going with Bill Buchanan to Texas to help buy some pot and bring it back for resale.

"They were on the road for two days and Bill Buchanan got to drinking. And he got to arguing and threatening when things didn't go his way. Steve Armstrong didn't like Bill Buchanan, and didn't like the way he was drinking and driving, and he told him so. Bill Buchanan stopped the car and said to him, 'Look man, you don't know who you're dealing with. I killed two men in Kentucky, and I don't mind killing two more. You lay off me, or you'll be sorry.'

"Bill Buchanan made one hell of an impression on Steve Armstrong. He scared him to death. Armstrong called his wife from Texas and told her what happened, that he was with crazy people, and that he was going to leave them and fly back home. After he got home he and his wife decided this was not the place for them and they left and found work someplace else.

"This guy, Steve Armstrong, is clean. No felony record. No record of any kind. He doesn't even know Frank Tamme. He didn't want to be involved with any of these people, he didn't want to testify – but he promised Diana Queen that he would, and he did. Steve Armstrong doesn't believe Tamme killed the two guys, he believes Bill Buchanan did.

"The circuit judge has now held three hearings on this. Diana Queen gave her full investigative report by affidavit. Steve Armstrong testified in person, and he told his story, and made a hell of a good witness. Frank Tamme testified on his own behalf and he told the judge his whole story.

"The judge listened to all this, and asked questions. At times you could tell she was having trouble believing what had happened to Frank Tamme in his two trials. She seemed incredulous."

Kenyon Meyer looked at me and ended his story, saying, "It's all in the hands of Judge Mary Noble now. She is making her decision and writing her opinion. It shouldn't be too long, but we don't know."

Here was the case. Here was a guy on death row for seventeen years, tried, convicted and sentenced to death twice, and he never had a chance to tell his own story. The jury never heard who Bill Buchanan really was and what he had to gain from his testimony, nor had they heard from an independent witness that Bill Buchanan had admitted killing two men in Kentucky.

What better case could there be to show the death penalty system didn't work? The miracle was clearly Father Richard Sullivan, who gave his inherited savings to an investigator out of his belief in the innocence of his boyhood friend.

If the circuit court decided it right we had our innocent man. We didn't know yet. We were going to have to wait to see if we had our miracle.

7

INTO THE FRAY

The 2000 Kentucky legislative session was set to commence the first week in January. It would continue for sixty working days, usually Monday through Friday of each week, except for the Martin Luther King holiday, January 19 and President's Day, February 16. For lobbying purposes Mondays and Fridays were difficult because most legislators arrived late on Monday, just in time for the legislative session, and they left as early as possible on Friday to get home for the weekend. It was Tuesday through Thursday when we had the best opportunity to meet with legislators.

Much of the groundwork for the 2000 session had been accomplished the previous year. We analyzed the members of the House and Senate the best we could with the information we had. I started keeping a little book on politicians, a black imitation leather address book I found in a drugstore and converted for this purpose. It was too big to fit in a pocket, but it carried easily and was handy.

In the black book I listed the name and basic personal and professional information available on each representative and senator, with notes on how each had voted on previous key bills, such as The Racial Justice Act. I noted what had been said of interest in our meetings, and in time my little black book became our ultimate reference tool.

There had been death penalty abolition bills filed in previous Kentucky legislative sessions but they had gone nowhere. No abolition bill had made it out of the Judiciary Committee, and in fact no abolition bill I knew of had ever been brought up for a vote in committee or on the floor of the house or senate.

We had been in contact with many of the members of the House and Senate Judiciary Committees either in person or on the telephone during the summer and fall. They knew we were becoming more active, and we were getting commitments from a few.

I headed for Frankfort practically every Tuesday, Wednesday and Thursday. We met with legislators and planned strategy. Because of the lobbying I did in 1998 helping Pat with The Racial Justice Act I knew my way around the capitol some, but now as I was getting in full swing I realized how green I was and how little I knew about how things worked. Time would cure that.

Pat suggested we meet with Representative Bob Heleringer, Republican of Louisville, and ask him to be the principal sponsor of the abolition bill. I did not know Representative Heleringer but Pat had worked with him on a number of issues for many years, and I followed his advice.

Bob Heleringer saw us not long thereafter and we sat down in his cubbyhole office and talked about the legislative session. He was a slender, dark-haired, nice-looking man in his late forties; a lawyer in Louisville as well as a state representative. Over a period of time I got to know him well although I don't know that we ever became friends. His political views were very conservative and perhaps the only social issue we agreed on was the abolition of the death penalty.

He had a self-effacing manner and a natural knack for the comedic.

Pat's rationale in going to Representative Heleringer was, I surmised, the advantage of a conservative leading the charge, rather than a well-labeled liberal. The dedication he brought to the issue was impressive.

Bob Heleringer was a German Catholic who opposed the death penalty on moral and religious grounds. He believed life was sacred, that life belonged to God, and that killing was a sin whether it was done by a murderer or by the state. It did not matter to him whether the victim was a fetus or a murderer. He was solid pro-life at both ends of the spectrum. He had neither use nor sympathy, nor interest in, a murderer; but he did not want him or her killed.

Because he was a Republican from an urban area in a House of Representatives dominated by rural Democrats, Bob Heleringer had no illusions about his power or influence. He went his own way, deciding each issue on his conservative philosophy, speaking up for what he believed, and taking victory or defeat stoically.

He was respected for his gentle manner and his consistency, and he agreed to be our leader for abolition of the death penalty in this session.

Our coalition also became a part of a larger group interested primarily in juvenile issues. In Kentucky, a juvenile as young as sixteen who committed a capital offense could, if convicted, be given the death penalty. This abomination aroused not only our interest but also that of the Kentucky Department of Juvenile Justice, the Department of Public Advocacy, Kentucky Youth Advocates, child psychologists, and a host of civic and religious groups.

They were a loosely organized coalition headed by Ernie Lewis, the executive director of the Department of Public Advocacy, who had lots of organizational and political savvy. This coalition supported a bill to abolish the death penalty for juveniles by raising the eligibility age from sixteen to eighteen. They looked for our support but were careful not to get engaged in the controversy over the abolition of the death penalty for everyone. Their emphasis was not the immoral irrationality of the death penalty, but that juveniles did not have the mature judgment to be held responsible for their acts to the extent of killing them, as we might adults.

For the Coalition to Abolish the Death Penalty this

argument, of course, begged the issue, but we supported the juvenile group in every way they asked.

A bill to abolish the death penalty for juveniles, sponsored by Representative Eleanor Jordan, Democrat of Louisville, was filed and became House Bill 311. Our bill to abolish the death penalty was filed by Representative Heleringer, and was House Bill 514. Both were assigned to the House Judiciary Committee.

Unexpectedly in early January both campaigns received a considerable boost from outside the Commonwealth. Illinois Governor George Ryan announced a moratorium on all executions in his state. Independent investigators and court actions disclosed that thirteen men on Illinois death row were either innocent or had been wrongfully convicted during a period when the state executed twelve individuals. This was too lopsided, even for a conservative Republican pro-death penalty man like George Ryan. He stopped the executions and set up a study panel. These events received great publicity in Kentucky and throughout the country and energized the debate on the pros and cons of the death penalty.

The second bit of good news came from New Orleans, where Sister Helen Prejean, author of *Dead Man Walking*, announced she was coming to Kentucky and would appear with us in support of abolishing the death penalty and in support of the juvenile bill.

Sister Helen Prejean was much in demand for a number of causes in Kentucky but we were able to schedule her for almost half a day. We planned a lunch in Frankfort in her honor and invited key legislators and supporters to attend. We set up a press conference in the capitol rotunda for 1:30 and made an appointment for Sister Helen to meet with Governor Paul Patton following the press conference.

I thought the arrangements were all very good and I looked forward to meeting Sister Helen Prejean. Her book and the movie that followed, had made an enormous difference in the public's attitude about the death penalty, and she continued to work for abolition giving speeches and meeting with legislators throughout the country.

I went early to the Holiday Inn downtown where we were having the luncheon and the private room and reception area were all ready and people were arriving.

There were many familiar faces and much milling around and I asked, "Has Sister Helen come yet? Where is she?" The person I was asking pointed and there she was right behind me on the telephone. She was a small woman with a kind but intense face.

When she was through she looked at me and said, "Who are you?" with the beginnings of a playful smile. I told her my name and she asked quickly, "Are you the man who wrote that wonderful book?" I nodded my head and felt such pleasure that she even knew about my book that I did not have the courtesy or presence of mind to respond, "You are the woman who wrote a much more wonderful book." But we talked, and she was extremely gracious.

The lunch went well, but it turned out to be a difficult time for legislators and only Representative Bob Heleringer showed, and he was late.

After lunch we hurried to the capitol. The rotunda was full of reporters, TV crews, and supporters for our press conference. The emphasis for this press conference was not only Sister Helen Prejean, but also families of murder victims.

One of our most powerful coalition partners was Murder Victims Families for Reconciliation (MVFR). Their members had suffered a loss through violence but did not want the murderer to be executed. Each individual in this group had a riveting personal story to tell that included the decision that killing for killing did not abate the loss.

Pat and I, with Renee Cushing and Maria Hines, leaders of MVFR, each spoke to our supporters and the press on current issues. The final speaker was Sister Helen, who was clearly our impressive star. She did a wonderful job telling of her ministry, her book and the movie, and the reasons she supported abolition.

When the last interview was done and the press was packing up I took her by the hand and said, "Come on, we're going to see the governor."

The governor's office was only a marble corridor from the rotunda, so we were soon in his gracious reception room, where we waited. The reception area had gorgeous scenes of Kentucky on the walls and people were busily coming and going, and everyone was as pleasant and smiley as possible.

A young woman came from the inner office, greeted us warmly, and asked if we wanted coffee. We didn't and she said the governor would have time to talk with Sister Helen in just a few minutes.

We waited some more. The woman later came back and said the governor wasn't going to be able to have the talk, but they would have time to have their picture taken together in a few minutes.

We waited. Finally the woman came back and said the governor would not be able to see us at all, and she was sorry.

We left, certainly no wiser. Why hadn't they just told us that in the first place?

We thanked Sister Helen for all she did, and she hurried off to her next engagement.

We continued raising money with some success and most fortunately the American Civil Liberties Union awarded us a $25,000 grant for our program. We kept our operating expenses low. Everyone except Kaye was a volunteer, and her pay was so modest much of what she did could be called volunteering. We decided to use the additional money to add an advertising component to our campaign.

We selected the districts of eight key legislators and recruited individuals from these districts who gave personal testimony about why they were opposed to the death penalty. We captioned the one-eighth page ads "DON'T KILL FOR ME." Each contained a picture of the local person and a paragraph about his or her reasons for opposing the death penalty. We ran the ads in the local daily and weekly papers in the eight districts and I thought we got a good response. The affected legislators were certainly aware of them as we found out, and the ads helped in recruiting members and volunteers.

Back in the legislature we followed the schedule we had laid out. Representative Heleringer and other supporters approached Representative Gross Lindsay about a hearing for our two bills, HB 514 and HB 311. At the same time all of us worked on all the committee members to get commitments for our two bills.

Even with the Kentucky legislature in session the invitations for us to speak and participate in forums or debates did not abate. I lived through two more radio talk shows, two good TV interviews, and a couple of speeches. We encouraged universities and civic groups—anyone who asked us—to hold forums or debates. They were an effective way for us to get our points across. Sponsors had increasing difficulty recruiting people to take the other side, supporting the death penalty. Commonwealth attorneys and other local prosecutors were the obvious targets, and most favored the death penalty, but few had the time or inclination to appear publicly and argue the issues.

One individual who was willing to be involved though was Jo Ann Phillips, executive director of Kentuckians Voice for Crime Victims. I was scheduled to appear on a forum with her in late January in a church basement in the suburbs of Louisville. I prepared for this occasion carefully.

I realized when it came to killing, or belonging to a family hurt by killing, I did not know what I was talking about. This was outside the realm of my experience. I remembered listening to Paul Stevens' story of the murder of his daughter, Cindy, trying to imagine how he felt, the emotions he had to face, and I didn't know how to do that. This was a whole different world, and because I had not experienced it I tried to be thoughtful and considerate of those who had.

The forum was in the early evening and when I arrived

people were already gathering. There were between twenty to thirty when we began. I met Jo Ann Phillips for the first time and she was a cordial, handsome blonde woman, carefully coiffured and self-possessed.

Kentuckians Voice for Crime Victims was organized a number of years ago in response to the lack of consideration given to crime victims by government and by society. They worked hard and effectively to promote crime victims' rights and to pass legislation requiring local law enforcement officers and prosecutors to keep victims informed about, and able to participate in, the prosecution of their assailants.

The organization had no official position for or against the death penalty, but that didn't deter Ms. Phillips. She lost her own daughter to murder and she said she believed that the death penalty was the punishment the killer deserved. During the forum Jo Ann Phillips had an outwardly calm and measured approach, but she was strong for the death penalty, and once she got going she had little reluctance to stretch the facts. Her stringent position strongly suggested that all the members of her group were for the death penalty, which was not the case.

I made the usual points in my presentation but spent time on my agreement with victims' families' rights and my respect for their opinions and their wishes. I did point out that many victims' families were members of Murdered Victims Families for Reconciliation that strongly opposed the death penalty, and the reasons for their position.

When we were through and all the questions asked and answered, I felt good about supporting abolition but still respectful to those who disagreed, particularly those who had suffered a loss in their own family.

Ms. Phillips and I parted amicably, but just before I left a woman from the group supporting Ms. Phillips appeared suddenly in front of me. Her eyes and face angry and close, she said with considerable vehemence, "How DARE you show disrespect for the memory of my daughter."

I answered simply, I was sorry; I didn't intend to show disrespect.

She turned and left quickly, and it occurred to me it probably didn't make any difference what I had said. For this woman, to favor the abolition of the death penalty was an insult to her dead daughter. What a sad thought that seemed.

• • • •

Pat and I continued with our public appearances and meeting with any legislators who would give us some time. When the Republicans became the majority party in the Senate, David Williams from Manchester was chosen President of the Senate, and basically he ran the show. I knew he was for the death penalty, but I needed to find out how much of an issue it was with him, and how likely he might be to go out of his way to stop us. His assistant indicated Williams would likely have a few minutes before a committee meeting if we wanted to give it a try. I was game, and I told him we would do it.

Outside his office there was a pleasant enough reception room with a couch and a few chairs and two desks opposite each other where the receptionists/legislative assistants were busy with their computer work. I took a seat.

I might not get to see Senator Williams, but it was worth taking a chance so I was prepared to sit for a while. I had read the paper, so I was just musing to myself.

The door from the hall sprang open with alarming suddenness and a short fat fellow bounded into the center of the room. He had a flushed clown's face, button nose, wide smile, and below it a green shirt and a red multi-design tie held by a cross tie pin with the inscription, "I LOVE JESUS."

The whirling dervish stopped and smiled upon one of the receptionists, who said, "Hi there, Bo, what you been doin'?"

Bo was Representative J. C "Bo" Ausmus III from Eastern Kentucky, a chiropractor, and one of the leaders in bringing us back to a Christian society.

Bo was ready for the question, and as he answered he began a little jig, lifting one foot and then the other, arms swinging, "Well, I've been puttin' up the Ten Commandments in schools and on court house walls; been to Louisville and had a big debate on radio with some of those liberal radical fellows; been back home, seen some patients, done some adjustments; and now I'm here to legislate. I am a busy man!"

As Bo was chanting all this news and swinging around with his red tie flying, he suddenly saw me sitting back on the sofa, watching him with a big grin.

Bo slowed his whirl as he recognized me and without taking a breath he continued, "YOU"—pointing his finger at me— "YOU...I seen you on TV...I seen you at the abolition rally. YOU are the greatest presenter...YOU are the most positive feller...YOU are the best I have ever seen."

Bo, and now the two receptionists, looked at me like the second coming. I felt the warmth of Bo's praise and prepared to respond...Bo, who hadn't yet taken a breath, announced loudly and prophetically, "I'm dead against you!" and he was out the door, gone.

The two receptionists and I, remnants of a tornado, had witnessed full blast Christian energy in Technicolor. I lost any idea of talking with Senator Williams. I silently, almost solemnly, shook hands with each of the two women and left. This, truly, was another world.

• • • •

We continued our pursuit of Judiciary Committee votes for House Bills 514 and 311. Bob Heleringer and Eleanor Jordan spoke to Gross Lindsay whenever the opportunity arose, asking him to call up the two bills for committee consideration. At the conclusion of a brief conversation one day in the hallway outside his office, Gross Lindsay said to Eleanor Jordan, "I'm scheduling those two bills for our meeting on February 17." That was all he said, no elaboration, and Eleanor Jordan reported back to us with a great smile on her face.

We were finally getting our hearing. There would be a debate, there would be a decision. We would find out if we truly had a majority in the committee for one or both of our bills. It seemed easy now. We had kept urging and pushing and asking, and it had happened. We were going to make some history.

We had over two weeks to get ready. Pat and I met with Bob Heleringer and Eleanor Jordan and Ernie Lewis to plan our strategy and what testimony we would present at the hearing in support of the two bills.

I was pleased to have the opportunity to work with Representative Eleanor Jordan. She was a liberal from Louisville but I knew her more by reputation than by personal experience. She was the only African-American woman in the legislature and it had taken some doing for her to get there.

Eleanor Jordan has the face of one who had never had a problem in the world: pleasant, smooth and rounded features, with nary a wrinkle. She was not a large woman but she held herself tall with a deep dignity. She had a beautiful smile and an open friendly approach to most every situation. However, I'd seen her angry, and the energy and fire that flared was impressive.

Eleanor Jordan got off to a tough start. She got pregnant and had a boy when she was eighteen. She was a single mother, and much later when she was an elected official and poverty issues came up, she said to the men sitting around, "Look, guys, I've been on welfare, I know what this is like." They listened.

As a young woman she took an interest in the poor neighborhood that was her home and became active when historic sites nearby were scheduled for demolition. She won some battles with city hall for preservation and this changed her views about her role in the world. Along the way she remembered an elementary school field trip when the class visited the state capitol. Looking down from the House of Representatives gallery she saw no one who looked like her. Eleanor Jordan ran for the House of Representatives from her district, and she won.

She was fun to work with and the five of us began to plan for our hearing. We did not know how much time we would be allowed. There were two bills to be considered so we assumed it would be an hour and we agreed we would split it between the two. Eleanor and Ernie would plan their presentation on raising the age for juvenile execution; Pat and Bob Heleringer and I would plan for abolition.

I wrestled with the question of how we could best use our thirty minutes. Our emphasis had to be on impressing the undecided votes on the committee, rather than the public or the press. Our first speaker would be the bill's sponsor, Bob Heleringer. That was a given, and it was a great way to begin our presentation. Bob said he needed about five to seven minutes, which would fit fine. I was sure he would speak eloquently on the issue of morality.

There were so many other issues on abolition that needed or could be covered; it was difficult to decide what emphasis would be most effective.

We had the case of Frank Tamme—our innocent man on death row—but the Fayette Circuit Court had not yet ruled on the issues that had been presented pointing to Frank Tamme's innocence.

We had the strong testimony of Maria Hines and Paul Stevens about their tragic loss due to violence and that the death penalty was not the answer.

We had the increasingly pertinent argument about the cost of the death penalty and the affect it was having on stretched local and state budgets. We had the contested issue of the death penalty as a deterrent, and our arguments about poor defense lawyers, and the unfairness of the proceedings. And always in this legislature we had the issue of religion and the strong support we had from the Kentucky Council of Churches, the Catholic Church, and the Jewish community.

After determining which committee members we

particularly wanted to impress we decided the best use of our time would be on the innocence issue, and on victims' families opposing the death penalty. On the innocence issue, the dramatic facts uncovered in the Frank Tamme case were still fresh in our minds. I thought Father Dick Sullivan and attorney Kenyon Meyer would each make great witnesses. Victims' families' testimony would be a powerful anticipation of, and response to, our opposition. We assumed the testimony from those supporting the death penalty would come from commonwealth attorneys relating grisly stories of murderers they prosecuted, and from Jo Ann Phillips of Kentuckians Voice For Crime Victims.

Nancy Jo Kemper of the Kentucky Council of Churches agreed to express the support of the religious community and we could call on Dr. Gary Potter of Eastern Kentucky University, an expert on death penalty statistics, to talk about deterrence.

We planned it out. Five minutes for Bob Heleringer, five for Kenyon Meyer, four for Dick Sullivan, and five for either Maria Hines or Paul Stevens speaking for victims families, three for Nancy Jo Kemper, and five for Gary Potter. This left us a little wiggle room for committee questions and unexpected interruptions. Eleanor Jordan and coalition members for the Juvenile Bill would likewise decide on their witnesses and plan the use of their time.

Several members of the Judiciary Committee, in addition to Bob Heleringer, were fundamentally opposed to the death penalty and needed no further convincing. One was Rob Wilkey, vice chair of Judiciary. Our problem with Rob Wilkey was whether he would stand up, if necessary, against the chair, Gross Lindsay. My guess was he would not.

Another member of the Judiciary Committee who strongly opposed the death penalty was Kathy Stein, Democrat from Lexington.

Kathy Stein was one of only a few women in the Kentucky legislature, one of only a very few liberal Democrats, and the only Jew. I admired her greatly. She stood five foot two, with blonde hair, wide eyes in a round face lit frequently with a shy smile. She had a trial attorney's confident manner, and a guileless amazement about the adventures of her life.

Kathy grew up in Hurricane, in Wise County, Virginia. She lived in Hurricane because her widowed grandmother was there, and Kathy's mother, as the youngest of six, was responsible for taking care of her. She went to the Hurricane Baptist Church: her grandfather had built it.

The Hurricane Baptist Church was neither the Pentecostals, nor the snake handlers. It was conservative Southern Baptist, and it was pretty much the center of life in Hurricane for Kathy and her family. There was Sunday school, then eleven o'clock services, then Sunday evening services, and Wednesday night prayer, and Bible camp, and, of course, the summer church picnics. There was no liquor, little music, and no dancing, but there was plenty of preaching.

The summer Kathy was eleven a revival came to town and Kathy knew there was talk of it being time for her to join the church—to "receive the call." Kathy hadn't heard any call but she noticed her mother looking at her anxiously and she asked her best girlfriend what she ought to do. Her friend told her, "Kathy, I'm gonna do it, and if I'm gonna do it, you got to too." And so she did it. She was baptized into the Hurricane Baptist Church. She noticed when all the excitement was past that nothing had changed.

Kathy got married at nineteen, as was expected in Hurricane, and then Kathy got very ill, an event that changed her life. The local doctor told her she had leukemia and that she was going to die. Kathy stopped and really tried to think about life. She tried to examine her life in the new perspective of death, and one of her first decision in that examination was to question the doctor's opinion about her illness. She sought medical advice outside Wise County, Virginia, and found the doctor was wrong. She did not have leukemia and she was not going to die. It was too late for everything to go on as it had; she had changed.

Her next decision was to leave Hurricane and go to law

school at the University of Kentucky. Her husband said that was okay and she left, but their marriage didn't survive her absence. When Kathy graduated she was no longer married. She had no reason to go back to Hurricane so she stayed in Kentucky.

It wasn't easy getting started as a young lawyer, particularly as a young woman lawyer, but Kathy found work as a part-time Jessamine County public defender. She got married again and had her first child. That marriage didn't last and after the divorce she was a working single mother. Kathy struggled with her life, with raising her baby, with religion, and with loneliness. Difficult times though brought out Kathy's natural optimism, and at each step of her way, and particularly at the missteps, she became more aware of her own independence and her ability to survive.

One night around Christmastime she met Alan Stein at a party. They fell in love, they courted, and they got married. Thirteen years had now passed, at the time of this writing, and Kathy had added two children, converted to Judaism, and taken on a career in politics.

Her conversion to Judaism came first. Alan didn't want it, and the rabbi, very kindly but very firmly, opposed it, but Kathy was determined. The first time she had gone with Alan to the synagogue she felt a comfort, a spiritual belonging she had never experienced before. For her there was a relief in thinking of Jesus as a prophet, and to be free of the virgin birth, and the resurrection tenets, that had troubled her for so long.

With Kathy's insistence the rabbi relented and Alan had little choice but to agree. Kathy began a year and a half of Judaic studies until she was ready to take the Beit Dein examination by three rabbis. She passed. By the time of the ritual mikva she was eight months pregnant, and when the baby boy was born he had a Jewish mother.

Kathy's career in politics commenced in a much more serendipitous fashion. A good friend was elected county attorney of Fayette County—the first woman to hold that office—and she appointed Kathy director of Domestic Violence Prosecutions. The problems of domestic violence became Kathy's issue and she tumbled into it with all her energy and passion. She became not only the prosecutor but the spokesperson and community teacher. She spoke well in public, she could persuade, and she liked that.

In 1996 the legislative representative in Kathy's district in Lexington decided to run for the state senate, leaving his seat open in the House. Before he announced this decision he walked down the street one Sunday afternoon and visited his neighbors Alan and Kathy Stein, who were sitting on the porch swing when he arrived. They talked a bit and he told them of his decision to run for the Senate and that he wanted to recruit a good person to run for his House seat.

Alan Stein was active in civic and charitable causes in Lexington and was a well-known local person. As he listened he became excited with the idea of being asked to run for state office and he blurted out, "I am really flattered that you would think of me to run for the legislature. But, honestly, with my business and other responsibilities, I just don't think I could, or that I should take that on right now." There was a silence, and shuffling of feet, and the visitor said, "Alan, I understand that, but it really is Kathy I had in mind."

Kathy had opposition from a man she knew and liked, but she beat him handily, and became a new legislator in the 83rd session of the Kentucky General Assembly. A career was launched.

Kathy began her duties and she was eager, and attentive. She read the bills and resolutions before they were called on the docket each day. She quickly mastered the desk buttons that lit up the green for "YES," or the red for "NO." The electronic boards behind the Speaker's chair announced the votes of each of the one hundred representatives.

Early in Kathy's first session the clerk, in his steady monotone, announced, "A Resolution calling upon the Kentucky General Assembly to go on record supporting the posting of the Ten Commandments in Kentucky state buildings." The roll call board was open for cosponsors.

Without hesitation she tapped the "NO" button and watched as the big boards filled up with all greens, except for one red light opposite the name Stein, K. A silence descended, and she felt the hairs on the back of her neck stand up when she realized everyone was looking at her. For the first time it really struck her how different she was. She was not one of them.

It was later explained to Kathy that she did not have to vote "NO." If she did not want to cosponsor the resolution she could simply not vote and only the green lights would show. She was also told, by a representative who kept patting her as he spoke, that she could still withdraw her "NO" vote, and it would not be recorded. She thanked the representatives for their advice, and let her vote stand.

When we got to crunch time in the Judiciary Committee voting on the abolition bills I had no doubt about the steadfastness of Representative Kathy Stein.

8

THE 2000 HEARING

I prepared for the hearing as I would a jury trial. How best to put forth the story—brief, simple, and straightforward. How to anticipate the opposition and plant the seeds of doubt in their case. How to engage the committee (jury) so a majority would conclude what you wanted, and think it was their idea. This was old hat, and it was fun.

The thirty-minute limit, which we assumed, made the planning tough; but the realization we would finally have a debate and a vote, made it all seem very worthwhile.

We were set for Bob Heleringer to lead off, and he would be sincere, believable, and set a tone of high morality.

Next we would present the innocence issue. I called Kenyon Meyer and we met and prepared his testimony. He would be our young, good looking, white knight who volunteered to defend Frank Tamme after he lost two trials, and now had new and convincing evidence of Tamme's innocence.

When I called Father Dick Sullivan to ask him to testify to his personal history with Frank Tamme, he was excited we would have a hearing. When I told him the time and date, he replied in his soft southern accent, "Carl, I just don't know that I can be there."

Father Dick Sullivan and two priest friends had been saving and planning for years to go to Italy and the Vatican, and that was where he was going to be on February 17. Nothing was going to change that.

I did not want to alter our strategy nor lose the

effectiveness of Dick Sullivan as a witness, and I asked him if we could videotape his testimony before he left, and he said sure. We had five days.

I started looking for someone who would do it cheap, since we were low on money, but I wanted it done professionally, no home movies.

Our middle daughter, Araby, recommended her friend Dave Shulhafer with a film company, Videobred. I called him and discovered he had at least two sterling qualities. One, he cared about social issues and gave us a wholesale rate, and two, his people did quality work.

A cameraman, a technician, and I drove to Elizabethtown that Saturday and taped Father Dick Sullivan sitting on a small settee in the little living room of the rectory. It was so Currier and Ives we should have done it in sepia. For an hour and a half we rehearsed and taped repeated versions of Dick Sullivan's four-minute personal story of Frank Tamme. On the fifth tape we all thought it looked and sounded great, and that was it.

Nancy Jo Kemper, executive director of the Kentucky Council of Churches who was well known to the Kentucky legislature would testify to the support from the religious community. We recruited Dr. Gary Potter, Professor of Police Studies at Eastern Kentucky University, who had collected data from across the country demonstrating the death penalty was not a deterrent, and he was a strong abolitionist.

Our closing was the story of murder victims' families and their opposition to the death penalty. After a lot of discussion we decided to use Paul Stevens. He had to travel a long way from western Kentucky, but he was willing to do it. His honesty came across so well and his story was such a profound triumph over loss that his completing our presentation would pose a serious obstacle for whatever the opposition had to say.

We were ready to present our case. Kaye was busy organizing supporters from all over the state to come to Frankfort and fill the hearing room with abolitionists.

The morning of the Judiciary Committee hearing dawned clear and cold. The committee met at twelve noon so we had the morning to garner our witnesses and greet our supporters. The hearing room was on the first floor of the Capitol Annex, large and plain. The committee members sat behind desks on two raised tiers against one wall and metal chairs lined much of the remaining floor space. Members of the press and TV knelt and sat in an area immediately in front of the committee and around the table reserved for witnesses.

We scheduled our volunteers to fill the room at about 11:15 a.m. and save the front row seats for our principals. The room had about 120 seats and standing room along the walls and in the back, and by 11:50 a.m. it was filled with supporters wearing "DON'T KILL FOR ME" stickers; we began spilling into the adjacent room that carried the committee proceedings on a television monitor.

Mid-morning I found the technician responsible for the video equipment in the hearing room and he took my tape of Father Dick Sullivan and set it up to be shown to the committee on my signal. He would be there to start the film and adjust the sound.

We were as ready as we were ever going to be. Pat, Kaye, and I took our seats near the front and watched as the committee members began to come in, get coffee, and start milling around. I was used to the punctuality of court proceedings and was surprised committee hearings rarely started on time. We waited while the committee members gathered.

The committee's agenda for the day was available at the sign-in table by the door and I picked up a copy and now had time to look at it. There were five bills listed before ours; we were last on the docket. Above our bills was a notation, "Each side will be allotted 30 minutes total for both of the following bills—HB 311, HB 514." We were not going to get our hoped-for hour.

The chairman, Gross Lindsay, came in and took his seat in the center at the top tier and nodded to his fellow committee members around him. When he counted a quorum it was almost 12:15. He banged his gavel and asked the secretary to call the roll. This she did and announced a quorum was present, and the committee session began.

From his perch, Gross Lindsay squinted over his glasses at the crowd in the room. "We welcome all of you to this committee meeting and I'll remind you there will be no disturbances from the spectators. That only takes time away from everyone else. If you've brought in signs, sit on them. The committee doesn't need signs to tell them how to vote."

With that he paused and looked us over and appeared vaguely displeased. On our instructions none of our supporters had brought signs into the room, other than the stickers they all wore prominently on their shirts or jackets.

"We'll start the meeting with House Bill..." he began calling the bills from the agenda list.

The representative sponsoring a called bill stood and came forward to a table and a microphone in front of the committee and explained the provisions of his bill and its purpose. The chair then asked if any committee members had questions. When the questions were concluded the chair looked about at his committee members and asked, "What is your pleasure?" A member moved for approval of the bill, then a second, and a vote was taken.

Some bills were held over for questions to be answered, or referred back for language changes or further discussion. I had the feeling most of the committee member anticipated what was going to be said, and knew what was going to happen.

The procedure went on and on and we all sat there trying to contain our anxieties. The committee session was scheduled from twelve to two and the time was running. It got to be one, and a little after, and then they got to us. Chairman Lindsay said, "I'm now going to call the death penalty bills, House Bill 311 and House Bill 514. We'll give you people for each side about thirty minutes," and without pausing or taking a breath the committee chairman announced matter of factly, "These bills will not be voted on today. We will decide at a later time if these bills will be posted and voted on."

I could feel the air being sucked out of my lungs. I looked at the chair in disbelief. The bills had been posted. Why would we go through this if there were not going to be a vote? I had no answer, only numbness. I listened as the chair continued, "Representative Jordan, your bill is House Bill 311, are you going to lead off?"

Our plan had been to start with the abolition bill, HB 514, and then move to the specific juvenile bill, HB 311, but Representative Jordan moved up to the witness table, and Bob Heleringer, sponsor of HB 514, said nothing, and so it went.

Eleanor Jordan brought Ernie Lewis of the Department of Public Advocacy with her and they sat at the witness table facing the committee.

Representative Jordan addressed the committee, looking over her large black-rimmed spectacles she slid to the end of her nose. She was a handsome woman and she spoke directly and effectively from her heart. She thanked the committee for the opportunity to present her bill and she explained the purpose was to raise the age for a capital offense from sixteen to eighteen and to make the maximum penalty for a juvenile life in prison for a minimum of twenty-five years.

When Eleanor Jordan concluded her remarks she introduced Dr. Ralph Kelly, commissioner of the Department of Juvenile Justice. Dr. Kelly was a professional in the juvenile justice field, an African-American brought in from another state several years ago to create the Department of Juvenile Justice. He took his seat at the table and began to read from prepared remarks. He had appeared before the Judiciary Committee many times previously and it seemed to me he had an edge in his testimony, and not a lot of patience with the workings of the legislative process.

He started off advising the committee that Kentucky's existing law permitting the execution of juveniles placed us in the company of Iran, Pakistan, Nigeria, and Saudi Arabia. He followed that with a discussion of international human rights laws and the assertion that any juvenile death penalty was blatantly racist. He found, I thought, a way to annoy, in one way or another, every member of the committee.

Eleanor Jordan spoke once again and as she introduced her next witness it occurred to me she was following the old schedule where she had thirty minutes instead of splitting the shortened period the chair was allowing us. At this rate Representative Jordan and the juvenile bill would use all the allotted time.

I asked myself if it really mattered since the committee was not going to vote on either bill. Yes it did matter. This was our hearing and we wanted a chance to have our say. But I was powerless to remind Eleanor Jordan to save us some time. The only person who could do that was Bob Heleringer and he sat silently in his chair in the committee. I was just a guy in the crowd.

Representative Jordan next brought Dr. Kerby Neill to the table to testify and he came forward: tall, slim, heavy eyebrows, looking calm and serious. Dr. Neill was a Lexington psychologist specializing in the problems of youth and violence. While he looked professorial he also had an aura of kindness, gentleness, about him.

He went directly to his message. The judgment of young people sixteen to eighteen years old is not always good, and that is often reflected in our laws. Individuals may not enter into contracts until they are eighteen, can't buy liquor until twenty-one, join the service until eighteen, and so on. To apply the ultimate penalty of death to those unable to exercise mature judgment and understand the consequences of their acts is unproductive and unjust. I thought many members of the committee paid close attention to Dr. Neill.

I kept hoping Eleanor would end and save us some time, but she didn't. The next witness she called was Deb Miller, executive director of Kentucky Youth Advocates. She reminded the committee of the mission of Kentucky Youth Advocates and said once again what the others had said and finally was finished.

Then Eleanor Jordan asked Ernie Lewis to make comments, which he did, and then finally Representative Jordan made a few closing remarks, and thanked the chairman and the committee. She had used twenty-five minutes.

Representative Gross Lindsay looked up and said, "Alright, thank you Representative Jordan. Now, Representative Heleringer, House Bill 514. Will you please address the committee?" He said nothing about the time, which I thought was a good sign.

"Yes, Mr. Chairman," replied Bob Heleringer and he left his committee seat and came down to the witness table. As he passed me he grabbed my arm and whispered, "Come sit with me, I don't want to be up there alone." And of course I did, and sat in the chair next to him.

Bob Heleringer had written his remarks and he pulled the paper from his pocket and placed it on the table in front of him. He looked very good as he sat there and began his remarks. He wore a dark blue suit, very neat, and he projected himself in a fresh, healthy, most honest sort of way.

"Thank you, Mr. Chairman, and my beloved colleagues on the Judiciary Committee."

He began by reminding the committee of the history of the death penalty in Kentucky; how we had gotten along very well for thirty-five years without an execution, until very recently when there had been two. He suggested there was a whole new generation of legislators since the death penalty had been reenacted in 1976 and there was need for a whole new debate.

I watched and listened, and it occurred to me that after all these years this was probably the first chance Bob Heleringer ever had to speak his piece before the Judiciary Committee on his feelings about the death penalty.

He began to speak about what he felt, what he believed.

"The cause of western civilization had never been advanced by the killing of a human being. How can we ever justify doing that? I believe," he said solemnly, "to the height, and to the width, and the depth of my soul that we should abolish the death penalty." His manner as he spoke slowly and thoughtfully, the way he leaned forward and looked at the committee, there was no doubt about his sincerity.

"I don't come here to plead for the men on death row. I don't sympathize with any of them. I don't forgive them. This is for their God to do. I don't plead for their lives. I plead for ours, for the souls of the citizens of this state. When we kill, we are descending to the level of the killer. We are betraying the sacred Judeo-Christian heritage of our civilization. We are capitulating to the mores of a murderer. How can we teach our children that killing is wrong when we go out and kill the killers? When we execute a murderer we cheapen and devalue the lost life of his victim. We are simply wreaking revenge."

As Bob Heleringer made his plea he paused occasionally, looking intently at each committee member. At other times he raised his hands as if in supplication. His speech lasted three or four minutes and his deep voice resounded as he concluded, "I say to each of you, as a Christian, as a legislator, as a father, that I defend to the depths of my soul the dignity and the sanctity of human life, every human life. Thank you."

The chair's admonition of no disturbance from the spectators was forgotten and our supporters who had waited so patiently for this moment rose as one with wild applause.

Chairman Lindsay just stared and did nothing.

This was Bob Heleringer's moment. He did not care there wasn't going to be a vote; he finally had his chance to say his piece, to the committee and to the world.

As the applause subsided Bob Heleringer said, "Mr. Chairman, our next witness is Mr. Kenyon Meyer, an attorney who will tell the committee about the case of Frank Tamme, currently on death row."

Gross Lindsay replied, "You got five minutes."

So the time was not going to be extended. We had four

more witnesses and five minutes.

Kenyon Meyer understood the press of time and gave a truncated version of his experiences in the Frank Tamme case: how he had gotten the case at the last minute; managed to get a stay of execution; and then the good fortune of a new investigator finding a new witness to Tamme's innocence and damning evidence of a prosecutor's deal with the principal witness against Tamme.

I wasn't sure how long he took but when he finished Bob Heleringer continued on, "Mr. Chairman, our next witness is Father Dick Sullivan who is out of the country and can not be here but his testimony is on tape." I heard the chairman ask, with increasing irritation, "How long is the tape?" I signaled the technician to start the tape, and as Representative Heleringer was trying to respond to Gross Lindsay's question the hearing room was filled with the voice of Father Dick Sullivan speaking directly from the two large television monitors facing the committee and there was nothing the chair could do but stop and listen, with a heavy scowl on his face.

The tape came across beautifully. Father Sullivan, looking very priest-like, recounted his personal knowledge of Frank Tamme and the role he had played in paying for the private investigator. He concluded by earnestly asking each member of the committee to vote for abolishing the death penalty.

When the tape ended, the chair had clearly had enough.

"Alright, Representative Heleringer, your time is up, you've run over your time, and we must move on."

"Well, Mr. Chairman, I understand, but I want you and the committee to know that Mr. Paul Stevens came here all the way from Dawson Springs to tell you about the murder of his daughter and why he opposes the death penalty. And, Ms. Nancy Jo Kemper is here to tell you of the opposition to the death penalty of the churches in Kentucky, and finally Dr. Gary Potter is here from Eastern Kentucky University to testify that the statistics show the death penalty is not a deterrent to murder."

If this had been me or Pat saying all of this I am sure Gross Lindsay would have cut us off, but since it was a representative, Lindsay restrained himself until Bob Heleringer paused for breath.

"Alright, alright, Representative Heleringer, move on."

With this Dr. Gary Potter came to the witness table with a stack of papers containing all his statistics, and said, "I have copies for all the committee members," and Lindsay said in finality, "Give them to the clerk."

Our hearing was over and all in all I thought it was a complete mess. The very idea that the chair would deny us a vote, and then Eleanor would take up 90 percent of the time, was beyond me. I looked around the crowd of supporters and it was clear they shared my disappointment, and they probably blamed it on me. And why not!

The chair once again intoned, "Let's come to order, and we will proceed. I know there are people here who wish to speak against these two bills. Mr. Patton, I believe you want to be heard, and who else? Ms. Philips, all right."

Phil Patton who was president of the Commonwealth Attorney's Association came forward and with him was Jo Ann Phillips of Kentuckians Voice for Crime Victims. I did not know Phil Patton, but he had the reputation of being a reasonable man.

The decision of whether to seek the death penalty was a decision vested by Kentucky statute in the Commonwealth Attorneys. Regardless of what they personally might think about the death penalty, this was a power they were not going to give up. Phil Patton followed the party line but he certainly was no extremist.

I was pretty wrung out by what had already happened, but I listened to what Patton had to say, and once again wondered why any of us bothered since the chair had ruled out a vote on either of the bills.

"Mr. Chairman," Phil Patton began, "I speak on behalf of the Kentucky Commonwealth Attorney's Association in opposition to these two bills. Our experience tells us that occasionally there are some crimes so heinous, so unconscionable, that there is no penalty that can bring justice other than the ultimate penalty, death. This legislature should not decide that by striking the death penalty from the statutes, but under our system that decision should most properly be made by a jury."

He continued with the basic arguments for the death penalty, denying mistakes are made or the system is unfair. He sounded most reasonable in his brief remarks, and I got the feeling he personally didn't give all that much of a damn about the issue one way or another.

Then Jo Ann Phillips came on looking her usual handsome self. What caught my eye as she began to speak were her very large dangling earrings and large red-rimmed glasses.

"What we must learn to do, Mr. Chairman and members of the committee, is to get help to our children before they enter into this cycle of violence. We must stop the execution of juveniles by stopping young people from murdering."

I thought that was a hell of a plan, but she didn't provide us with any specifics.

Jo Ann Phillips continued talking about victims' rights and that the punishment should fit the crime and that a majority of Kentuckians wanted to keep the death penalty, and in her opinion the death penalty was the only way to end the cycle of violence.

That was it, and the chairman looked about the room and said, "The committee will discuss this further and see what we are going to do with these two bills."

I, and everyone else in the room, headed for the doors.

As I drove home it struck me that part of our problem, or certainly part of my problem, was the assumptions made. I had a tendency to take people and situations at their face value. It did not occur to me instinctively to look for hidden agendas or motives in the people I dealt with.

It never occurred to me Gross Lindsay could have a hearing

without taking a vote. Could I have anticipated it, and if I had what would I have done? To assume people will do what you think they should do is a pleasant way to proceed, but in my disappointment I realized I was more than a bit naive.

I met with Pat in Frankfort the following morning and we talked about where we'd go from here. Of course we couldn't abandon the cause. We outlined a strategy for the coming week: visiting each of the committee members we thought favorable to our bills and asking them to speak with Gross Lindsay about a vote. We also decided to go to the Democratic leadership in the House and see if they would put pressure on Gross.

The most memorable of our visits with committee members was with Representative Stan Cave, a Republican from Lexington, and a good legislator. He readily agreed to urge Chairman Lindsay to post the bills for a vote. When we suggested he make a motion at a committee meeting to put the two bills on the agenda for a vote, contrary to what Gross Lindsay had already said, Representative Cave looked at us as if we'd lost our minds.

"I'm for your bills," he said, "but it would be suicide to go against the chairman."

Well, there you have it.

9

DO YOU ACCEPT JESUS?

We continued to beat our heads against very hard walls on abolition issues while there were, of course, a lot of other issues and interests fighting for legislative attention. One of the easiest subjects to get front and center in the Kentucky legislature was religion—specifically permitting prayer in public schools and displaying the Ten Commandments in public spaces.

Kentucky's position on the separation of church and state was unique. Kentucky Revised Statute 158.180, passed by the legislature in the 1970s, mandated posting the Ten Commandments in every public school in the Commonwealth. Objecting parents took a case to the United States Supreme Court which unanimously held in *Stone v. Graham* that the law was an unconstitutional intrusion into religion by the Kentucky government. This Supreme Court case from Kentucky made it clear to the entire country that under the First Amendment the government's neutrality in religious matters precluded posting the Ten Commandments in public school rooms.

Fundamentalist ideas have a long life in these parts. To many, the posting of religious symbols, the mere physical act of doing it, brought satisfaction. The significance of the moral postulates, particularly if followed, was never debated, or possibly even thought about; it was only important they be seen.

When I learned the Ten Commandments bills were coming on the House floor for debate I signed for my pass to the chamber and climbed to the visitor's gallery to watch. Senate Joint Resolution 57 was the lead bill. It passed the Senate and was now on the House floor for debate. House Floor Amendment 18 on the Ten Commandment obelisk had been offered and was pending.

In the 1950s the Loyal Order of Eagles gave to the Commonwealth of Kentucky a monument inscribed with the Ten Commandments. The Eagles did this for a number of states with money donated by movie producer Cecil B. DeMille promoting his movie, *The Ten Commandments*. By some unknown authority the capitol grounds crew erected the large concrete thing outside the capitol.

There it stood, or sat, for a number of years, viewed by many passing legislators and tourists, until either objection or embarrassment, or some of both, caused officials to remove and place it in storage in the capitol basement. It was gone but not forgotten. House Floor Amendment 18, offered to Senate Joint Resolution 57 by Representative Tom Riner of Louisville would: "Require relocation on the capitol grounds of a monument on which the Ten Commandments are inscribed and which was previously displayed in the capitol grounds; require the monument to be made a part of an historic display, near the floral clock..."

The debate proceeded. Part of the undercurrent of all the debates on church-state separation in the Kentucky legislature is the painful memory of the money the state has been required to pay in cases won by the American Civil Liberties Union of Kentucky on this issue. There are many things abhorrent to Kentucky's legislators and making dollar contributions to the ACLU is way up there.

Another floor amendment was offered to SJR 57 by Representative Kathy Stein as House Floor Amendment 6, "Directing that the statues in the capitol rotunda (of Abraham Lincoln, Jeff Davis, Henry Clay, et al.) be sold, and that the proceeds be deposited in an account dedicated to the payment of legal fees incurred in defense of unconstitutional legislation enacted by the general assembly." Only a few members, other than Kathy, thought that was funny.

There was a general hubbub in the crowded chambers,

some legislators paying attention and others not. Off slightly to the corner of the chamber toward the back, Representative Billy Polston of Monroe County, District 53, stood up and the Speaker of the House, Jody Richards, said, "The chair recognizes the gentleman from Monroe 53."

Billy Polston stood tall and thin. He was getting gray and bald and was probably in his late sixties. He wore a neat dark blue suit, white shirt, and a fancy blue figured tie. His breast pocket showed a red handkerchief poking up neatly pressed, and he had a white carnation in his lapel. His eyes looked out under heavy shaggy eyebrows and over a large nose, and lean high cheekbones.

He spoke in a soft courteous tone. "Ladies and gentlemen of the House. I would like to address issues that's been bothering me a little lately, since I've been here. That's people talking about religion. Everything that comes up they want to oppose, it's religion. I am a firm believer in separation of church and state— a firm believer—a belief I'd lay down my life for, if I had to. That's why this country was founded. Because of the belief of the difference between church and state. Every time something comes up here we want to interject the church—well, the church has been torn into a million pieces. We can agree on things as long as we keep it out of religion. Religion has been instilled in our lives, and we can't just come up here and listen and change our views on religion. It takes years and years of teaching if you're gonna change somebody. This is something we can't do.

"Now, I support this posting of the Ten Commandments. I support it because I think it will help bring about—not division— but help us heal together, because I think that's what we need is some healing together, not only as a body here, making laws, but also as a religious body. And I want to say this, if I may. I would like to ask the lady from Fayette a question."

The Speaker of the House looked up, "The lady from Fayette 75, will you yield for a question?" This was Representative Kathy Stein, and she looked up and replied quickly, "I certainly will."

The Speaker—"Gentleman from Monroe 53."

"First of all," Billy Polston turned to his left toward Kathy Stein and gave a courtly nod to her as he continued speaking, "I want to say I think you're a good legislator. I respect you very much as an individual, and you've got all my respect, but I just want to ask you one question, and this is very personal...do you believe that Jesus Christ is the Lord and Savior of our lives?"

I could see Kathy Stein's eyes grow large, and she started talking almost reflexively as her mind must have been racing. "Gentleman from Monroe, I certainly will answer that personal question," and then came the pause. The chamber was absolutely silent. I looked at the Speaker to see what he would do, and he did nothing. No one said a word. Representative Kathy Stein looked directly at Billy Polston, and said:

"I believe that Jesus of Nazareth was a wonderful rabbi and teacher. I believe that every statement he made that has been passed down to us in the New Testament are very admirable rules to live by, but Gentleman from Monroe, the Jewish faith does not believe he was the Messiah. We wait upon the Messiah even in these days. We are getting ready to celebrate a very sacred holiday known as the Pesach, Passover, and in that we go through a liturgy that talks about Moses taking the people of Israel out of bondage and into the Promised Land. Part of that liturgy calls for the coming of the Messiah, as quickly as possible.

"In answering that, Gentleman from Monroe, and I have a great deal of respect for you, I hope that that does not offend you, and I hope that that does not diminish my stature somehow or another in your eyes. But, if nothing else, I will always be honest, Gentleman from Monroe."

When she finished there was a slight splatter of applause that quickly died of embarrassment.

Then the Speaker, "Gentleman from Monroe 53." Billy Polston smiled and looked all the world like a Baptist Sunday school teacher. Looking at Representative Kathy Stein he said, "May I ask you another question? I respect you very much, again for what you say. It will not offend me in any way what you say about religion, or about the body here, but I ask you once again, do you not believe that Jesus Christ was raised for our sins?"

Kathy Stein now seemed a little weary, slumped in her chair, "Gentleman from Monroe—no, I do not."

"I did not mean to embarrass you or anything like that but all this religion, people one way and people another way, and wanting to post the Ten Commandments – I am for posting. I want that to be publicly known. But I don't want religion, church and state, mixed up, or we'll all get down here so we can't agree on anything. We can't get involved in religion in this body or we'll fall. We've got to stay on statesmanship."

Billy Polston sat down. The Speaker was still standing behind the podium, gavel in hand, mouth open, looking bewildered. Kathy Stein sat in her chair motionless.

I left the gallery wondering how many times in the history of our republic a legislator had been asked if he or she accepted Jesus. Perhaps it was more times than I wanted to know.

• • • •

A few days later we got a call for a meeting of the ad hoc group concentrating on our bill to abolish the death penalty for juveniles. It was held in Representative Eleanor Jordan's office and Pat and I assembled with the others. When Representative Jordan appeared she did not seem happy.

"I asked you all to come so I can tell everyone what has happened, and so we'll all know. I had a meeting with Representative Gross Lindsay about the juvenile bill and bringing it to a vote in his committee. He is agreeable to posting the bill and having a vote, subject to the following conditions: The committee will amend the bill so that the final version will raise the age from sixteen to seventeen, rather than eighteen. Seventeen year olds would still be subject to the death penalty. And further, that sixteen year olds, while they won't be subject to the death penalty, will be subject to a sentence of life in prison without

116

possibility of probation or parole. These were the chairman's terms for posting my bill for a vote."

I thought, we do learn more about our chairman, Mr. Lindsay, every day.

"I told him," Eleanor Jordan continued quickly, "that these terms were not acceptable, and he said, 'Well, that's it. You either accept that, or it is nothing.'"

"I told him under those conditions, it would have to be nothing. As far as I am concerned, that's it. It is over for this session." I thought for a minute she was going to cry, but she didn't. And she was right, it was over.

10

WHAT'S NEXT?

Our campaign to abolish the death penalty in the 2000 legislature had a notable lack of political, social, or artistic success. In locker room talk, we got our ass kicked.

Fortunately, neither Pat nor I had much tolerance for morbidity. Our spirits recovered and as they did our attention was turned to the status of our coalition. Kaye brought us lists and figures, and we found that while we were stumbling around in the legislature our coalition had changed, and changed radically. Whether it was the speeches, the TV, the radio, the news coverage, or all of our failures, we did not know, but in the last six months the Kentucky Coalition to Abolish the Death Penalty had almost tripled its coalition partners. We now numbered forty organizations, and individual memberships had almost doubled.

Nothing succeeds like failure. We were becoming a real, viable organization for social change. We began to pick up the pieces and plan the next step in the campaign. The next regular session of the Kentucky legislature wasn't until 2002, a year and a half away, but there was the possibility of a short legislative session in 2001. A proposed constitutional amendment would be on the ballot in the November 2000 election posing the question: Should the Kentucky legislature meet in odd numbered years for a thirty working day session, commencing the first week in January?

The amendment was supported by a bipartisan coalition of political, civic, and business leaders to reduce the number of expensive special sessions called by the governor in recent years to decide issues for which there had not been time or inclination to resolve in the regular sessions.

Amending the Kentucky Constitution, as archaic as it was, was not easy. There was always strong suspicion and opposition to any change. Under the current constitution our legislature met for sixty days every two years. An old political saw had it that we'd be better off if the legislature met for two days every sixty years. It was that philosophy that the proposed amendment faced.

The annual membership meeting of KCADP was scheduled for June 10. Kaye, Pat, and I strove to plan something to relieve our member's minds of all our recent failures and give us cause to charge into a new day.

We chose the lodge at Kentucky's Natural Bridge State Park, a sensational site in the Daniel Boone National Forest, as our meeting place. We planned two-hour sessions before and after lunch to set the strategy for our next campaign and to further the development of our coalition.

About seventy people from all over the state showed up on a beautiful June day. When we were through we had gotten a number of good ideas, and joined in some fine story telling and good laughs with like-minded people.

One of the suggestions made in the workshops was to divide the state into eight geographical regions and recruit at least two coordinators to be responsible for each region. We were now large enough that this idea was feasible and over half of the needed coordinators volunteered from the attendees. We put this idea into place.

The principal challenge that came out of the meeting was the goal to be the first southern state to abolish the death penalty. That step would lead to other progressive social changes here and throughout the South.

Wishful thinking, but certainly invigorating.

There were several helpful developments that we began to work into our speeches and written materials. First were the results of several recent University of Kentucky public opinion polls on the death penalty.

Local polls consistently showed almost seventy percent of Kentuckians favored the death penalty for capital crimes; for the first time in the most recent UK poll the possibility of life without probation or parole was introduced into the questions. When asked to state a preference between the death penalty and life without probation or parole for capital crimes the seventy percent dropped dramatically to 31 percent, with 54 percent selecting life without parole. This, mind you, was not a vote against the death penalty, but the expression of a preference. It was obviously significant, and we began to use this information anyway we could.

Another poll in June 2000 included questions on the punishment of juveniles. When given the choice about whether sixteen and seventeen year olds should receive the death penalty or a prison term for a capital crime, almost seventy percent selected prison over the death penalty. I thought this was a no-brainer, but we found the information very useful in lobbying legislators.

The second development came like a thunderbolt. Late in August I received a call, early in the morning at home, from attorney Kenyon Meyer. He said he had just received a message from the clerk of the Fayette Circuit Court. Judge Noble had set aside Frank Tamme's conviction and death sentence.

I was bouncing up and down as I listened to Kenyon's excited voice. He only knew what the clerk had said, but they were faxing a copy of Judge Noble's order and opinion to him. He said he'd fax it to me, but hell, I didn't have a fax machine. I told him I'd come to his office.

By the time I got there he had received the order and opinion of the court and had made me a copy. The two of us sat in his office and read it.

The order set aside the second conviction of Frank Tamme, and granted him a new trial. We read the judge's opinion, which was four pages, and here are two statements from her opinion that sum it up pretty well:

"The Court is not unmindful that Tamme has already had two trials on these charges. A defendant cannot be given repeated attempts to 'get it right' absent extremely good cause. The court believes denial of a full defense to be extremely good cause even though the cost and delay is frustrating to the citizens of the Commonwealth and especially to the families of the victims. However, justice is not served if there is not reasonable certainty that the proper man is being punished. No victim's grief can be assuaged by the punishment or death of the wrong person....

"Any trial, but particularly one where a man's life is at stake, should reveal the truth. This can only be accomplished when both sides have the opportunity to present their story fairly, and the jury can judge based on this equity."

The court ruled that Frank Tamme never had that chance.

I looked at Kenyon Meyer, and this large man appeared about to burst with relief and happiness. I would wager he had never been that excited about a corporate case.

"What's next?" I asked.

"Well," he said, looking away and thinking for a moment. "What should happen is the attorney general should propose that Tamme plea to a lesser offense and be released on time served." He paused and looked back at me.

"But that in all probability won't happen. The attorney general will appeal directly to the Kentucky Supreme Court, put the case on a fast track, and pull out all the stops on the appeal on the basis that this was a horrible double murder and no defendant should have unlimited trials to try for an acquittal. I best start working on my brief."

Kenyon was learning the ways of the criminal justice system faster than most. In spite of his spectacular victory in circuit court I could tell he was wary and not sure of the future of his case.

"There is another element to this," he said looking at me solemnly, and I waited.

"Frank Tamme has hepatitis, type B. He probably got it in Vietnam. There are treatments for it, but we're not having much luck in getting any attention. The Department of Public Advocacy and Sister Chris and I are working on it, but you know, it's tough on death row.

"How sick is he?" I asked.

"I don't know," Kenyon answered, "except this is pretty serious stuff. I think, I certainly hope, this decision will help."

I thanked him for all he had accomplished, and he smiled and said we would keep in touch.

We now had a reversal of Frank Tamme's conviction and a clear decision that the system wasn't working. We could argue in good faith that Frank Tamme was innocent. The circuit court decision would be on radio and TV that evening and in the newspapers in the morning. I headed to our office and in my head I was preparing a new pamphlet, "Death Row's Innocent Man."

The story did get good play, but the reporters whom we'd briefed on this case wrote long and thoughtful, well-balanced articles that were about as exciting as an eel fight. I wanted headlines, "MAN ON DEATH ROW NOT GUILTY." I was dreaming.

Fall approached and we were presented with good news and bad news. The good news was that Pat was reassigned by the bishop from Catholic Charities to the Catholic Conference in Frankfort as a policy analyst. This meant he would have a lot more time to spend on abolition and would be much closer to the action. Pat, after all, was the abolition campaign and this was a real boost for us.

The bad news was we had to move our office. We found free space in the basement of the Episcopal Cathedral buildings in downtown Louisville. We had a number of Episcopalian leaders active in the abolition campaign, and they were all very accommodating.

Before we knew it the November election was upon us, and to my amazement the proposed constitutional amendment passed handily; we could start getting ready for another legislative session in less than two months.

I was glad the amendment had passed. I voted for it and I looked forward to going back to the general assembly. Under the terms of the amendment the session would be for only thirty working days so the likelihood of getting very far with controversial legislation, such as abolition, was slim, but even so, I was ready to get back at it. I believed if we kept up the lobbying, without taking the defeats too seriously, the justice of our cause would finally be recognized and all the barriers would be overcome.

At our first planning session an idea popped up that dramatically changed our lobbying strategy. Scott Wegenast, a policy analyst at the Catholic Conference, scratched his head in a deferential manner, and said, "You know, we have all these new members and volunteers, why don't we give them something to do in the legislature?"

Previously we had used our members to call and write their legislators in support of our bills, and we asked them to come to our press conferences and rallies.

"What I'm suggesting," Scott said, "is we organize them to come to Frankfort every day during the legislative session, and go see their legislators in person, and walk the halls; be a presence."

Why not? We looked at each other, hunched our shoulders in mock humor, and decided to try it. We marked off each Tuesday, Wednesday, and Thursday of the five-week session, put an announcement and a call for volunteers on our web site and in the KCADP Newsletter.

It didn't take long for the telephone to ring. The troops were interested in coming to Frankfort.

"I can come on Tuesday in February because I have the day off and I've always wanted to see what is going on in Frankfort."

"I will be there and I'll bring two sisters from the convent. Will you tell me what to say?"

The marked-off days began to fill with volunteers. Some days we had as few as two or three, but others we had eight to ten. Before we were through there wasn't a single designated legislative day we didn't have volunteers.

This of course meant that Kaye or Pat or I had to be there early each morning to organize, reassure, and lead the way. Actually, it had to be me mostly because by now Kaye had had a baby boy, Brendan, and Pat had a lot of other responsibilities. But that was all right. I was willing to give it a go.

January was soon upon us and the legislature began its first odd-year short session. There was so little time to plan that no one, neither Republican nor Democrat, nor the many lobbyists, knew quite what to expect.

Our plan was to get an abolition bill and a juvenile bill introduced as soon as possible. First, however, we had to reorganize our legislator sponsors because Eleanor Jordan had left the legislature to run for Congress, and Bob Heleringer was getting ready to retire and he felt he had about run his course.

For the juvenile bill we recruited Representative Jim Wayne to take a leadership role and work with a number of our regular supporters. Jim Wayne was an unusual man to be in the legislature. He was a tall, very slender gentleman, with a long, pale, and pleasant face. He was studious looking, serious, and shy.

We were talking one day and he said, "The truth is I've been thinking about social issues since I was a kid. My dad was a steward in the Fireman's and Oiler's Union at Seagrams Distillery. He'd talk about union problems at dinner. My mother was a registered nurse at St. Joseph's Infirmary and she would talk about her days. They had five boys, I was the middle one, and we would really get into it.

"I was always sort of interested in politics and volunteered some as a kid, but you know what, I never thought seriously about getting involved myself until college. I was at Maryknoll, outside of Chicago, when the 1968 Democratic Convention was held in Chicago, with all the war protests. A bunch of Maryknoll students were in the protests when the police riots started and some of my friends were arrested. The craziest thing happened. The president of the college, *the president* of Maryknoll, went down to the jail and personally bailed the students out. That really impressed me. Somehow, that made me realize these issues were important, and I needed to be involved.

"After Maryknoll I went to the seminary and thought I'd be a priest; but then I decided not to. I went to Smith College and got a master's degree in social work, and that's what I've been doing ever since, besides being in the legislature, of course."

Representative Jim Wayne worked for what he believed in and fortunately he was with us on abolishing the death penalty, particularly for juveniles. House Bill 109 for abolishing the death penalty for juveniles was introduced on January 4.

Representative Tom Burch, a strong advocate for abolition, introduced House Bill 122 on January 5 calling for the total abolition of the death penalty. We recruited Representative Mary Lou Marzian to take a leadership role along with Tom and our other supporters.

Representative Mary Lou Marzian generally moved quietly through the legislative process. She was affable, with a broad direct smile in a round Irish face. She tended to fiddle with the loose ends of her blonde hair when she was thinking or talking. I got to know her while lobbying and she was the kind of person the more you knew her the more there was to like and admire.

Her dad was Bill Kearney, a lawyer, and Mary Lou was the second oldest of the seven Kearney kids. She did well in parochial school and had lots of interests, but she said to me, "It wasn't until I was working on my degree at the University of Louisville I first began to realize how women were getting screwed."

"One eye-opener for me was attending a National Women's Conference. It was in Houston, when Jimmy Carter was president. One of my great teachers, Lillyalice Akers, took the whole class to Texas in a bus. All the important women were there. I remember particularly Gloria Steinem. I became a feminist."

125

Mary Lou Kearney became a nurse. She started as an RN at Jewish Hospital, began to specialize in renal therapy, and ended up the coordinator of the renal transplant program at the University of Louisville Hospital. She fell in love and married Bill Marzian, and they had a daughter, Nicki.

Mary Lou never thought about running for office until friends in the local National Organization for Women urged her in 1994 to run for a vacant seat in her state legislative district. This she did and she won.

"At first, you know, I was overwhelmed, and I was intimidated by all those guys in Frankfort. But when I heard some of the speeches they gave, I said hell, I can do better than that. My real interest in the beginning was just women's issues, but as time passed and I saw more of what was needed in Kentucky, my horizon broadened to include housing and jobs and particularly health care. My gender and my views always put me in the minority, but I just keep plugging away at it."

We were fortunate to have her leading the battle. Our two bills were filed, and we were ready to go. Each day we met the volunteers at 9:00 a.m. at the Catholic Conference office just outside Frankfort—a five-minute drive from the capitol. We provided coffee and doughnuts (except when I forgot) and for about thirty minutes we sat around the table in the small conference room and planned the day.

First I gave a short report on what was going on in the campaign generally and then outlined how we would spend our day in Frankfort. We had a one-page, front and back, instruction sheet and guide for our volunteers we reviewed together.

Each volunteer received the name, office, and telephone number of his or her representative and senator; the names and locations of the four major leaders in the House and the Senate; and, finally, the titles and numbers of the two principal abolition bills we were supporting.

Our basic instructions were: "We are all volunteer lobbyists. We don't have to register or anything. All we have to do is be polite, tell the truth, and convince our representatives that they should abolish the death penalty."

The plan was for volunteers to go first to the offices of their home representative and senator. They called first from our office to say they were coming and tried to make an appointment. They knew the bills and the talking points, and had the KCADP brochure to hand out. We also gave them the Frank Tamme, "Innocent Man of Death Row" flyer that could be distributed and discussed.

After visiting the offices of their own representatives, volunteers selected legislators who lived near them or most interested them and proceeded to those offices for a cold call. The pitch to leadership was that they as citizen volunteers and voters supported House Bills 109 and 122 and wanted leadership to see that these bills received a hearing and a vote in committee. If they couldn't see their target person they left personal notes and copies of our pamphlet and the Tamme flyer.

Beside pamphlets and flyers that were handed out freely, each volunteer wore a large round blue and white sticker on their coat or jacket declaring, "I OPPOSE THE DEATH PENALTY." We all stood out as we moved about the capitol annex. It was interesting to watch the reaction of passersby who first noticed the sticker and invariably looked curiously to see the wearer's face.

After the volunteers had been to see their legislators it was usually getting close to lunchtime. By prearrangement they went to several strategic corridors where many legislators had to pass on the way to and from committee meetings and to lunch. We wanted it to appear that there were a lot of us and that we were everywhere. Occasionally we heard comments that we were successful at this. One legislator said to me, laughing, "I think your people are following me."

At lunchtime we reconvened in the cafeteria in the basement of the annex. As we sat around a table eating lunch each volunteer reported on the morning adventures. It was fun to watch the people who sat so uneasily at the morning briefing, asking questions tentatively, worrying about keeping the facts straight, and finding the right offices, now bright and animated veterans of the legislative wars. Whether they were successful in getting their legislators to agree with them or not, or whether they even got to see and talk to them, there was something in the very act of demonstrating their beliefs and participating in the democratic process that was invigorating to each of them. It could be seen in their faces and heard in the excitement of their voices. They were pumped.

At one of our cafeteria rendezvous later in the session, six or seven of us sat around the table, four of whom were nuns who had come together. When the reporting and commentating was about done, a volunteer I didn't know asked me, "How did you get involved in this campaign?" I gave the short version, "The abolition of the death penalty is a major issue for the American Civil Liberties Union, and I got involved through being an ACLU member."

In most Kentucky circles mention of membership in the ACLU is followed by an awkward silence, as it was this time. I happened to glance across the table—one of the nuns furtively smiled, and mouthed silently, "So am I." I'm sure she could tell from the grin on my face how pleased I was.

After lunch the volunteers who had time went back to the offices of legislators they had missed. Shortly before two o'clock many of them walked through the tunnel from the annex to the capitol to watch the proceedings in either the House or the Senate at opposite ends of the ornate marbled third floor of the capitol. Each chamber had a gallery open to the public and the spectacle of legislative proceedings was often an interesting conclusion to their day of lobbying in Frankfort. When they got tired, or it was over, they left for home as I did, and another legislative day was over

The beginning and ending of my day in Frankfort was marked by the drive between Louisville and the capitol. I began early in the morning driving on River Road, next to the Ohio, and then on to I-64 going east to Frankfort. From my house to the Catholic Conference office was forty-six minutes, twenty-nine of which was I-64. If it were raining heavily, I added four to seven minutes to the total. Each morning I drove east with the planet's whirl, spinning into the sun rising in front of me. Each morning there was recognition of beginnings as I squinted into the fresh light. In the late afternoons when I headed home I was attached to the departing sun, moving against the planet's flow and toward the inevitable night. There was a beginning and an ending embracing me every day on my highway.

Pat and I routinely undertook to visit with newly elected legislators as early as possible, to offer a welcome and make a good first impression for the campaign. In this short session one of the newly elected members was Stan Lee from Lexington. We knew he was a lawyer and listed himself as "Christian," and had been assigned to the House Judiciary Committee.

Our information came from the official book of legislators published by *The Kentucky Gazette*. This fat little book was an essential tool for lobbyists. Each senator and representative had a separate page with a picture and vital statistics, including his or her plurality in the last election, and how much money had been raised and spent. Religion was considered vital information, and members listed "Baptist" or "Methodist," and there were a number of "Catholics." Only one or two left that space blank. When the denomination was listed as "Christian," it usually meant the Church of Christ, or the Disciples of Christ.

We had no trouble in scheduling an appointment with Representative Lee and though he wasn't a Catholic Pat went with me so we could press him on both the secular and the religious fronts.

Stan Lee was a pleasant, intense looking man in his early forties who greeted us politely and seemed a little lost in his cubbyhole office with its unpacked boxes, bare walls, a bare desk and computer. We made nice talk; how did he like it so far, were his committee assignments okay, that sort of thing, and he was quick to share his first impressions with us.

After a bit, I began to outline our campaign and the basic reasons Kentucky would be a less violent state if we abolished the death penalty, and he listened. Along the way I asked if he had received the complimentary copy of my book we had sent. He replied, yes, indeed he had, and he laughed as he said he gave it to his wife to read, as she might be more receptive.

Pat took it up at that point and began to talk about the position taken by the various Christian denominations and about how this religious anti-death penalty movement had developed. Very suddenly our new legislator interrupted; it was such an abrupt change. His eyes were very dark. Both his hands were raised in the air as he started speaking.

"All your worries, all your concerns, will soon be over," he announced solemnly.

We stopped and waited. He stared at us intently.

"With the coming of Christ, there will be a circle of Judges who will decide...who is good, who is evil...and," (looking at us knowingly) "there will be NO APPEAL. Then there will be a thousand years of goodness—of bliss!" His voice trailed off, his head now raised, and he looked off in the distance.

We stared. This proclamation of judgment was not put forth for debate. It was Representative Stan Lee's answer to our concerns about the death penalty. He was saying it didn't matter. We were stunned. Pat nervously got up, and I think he mumbled something, and the two of us left. Representative Lee was not a likely ally on the House Judiciary Committee.

As we hastened down the corridor it came to me that it was less than a day's walk from Representative Lee's home in Central Kentucky to a place called Cane Ridge. This fact came tumbling in my mind as I replayed Representative Lee's ringing proclamation of the coming of Christ, the judging of the good and the evil, and the millennial joy promised in the Book of Revelations. This was straight out of the Cane Ridge revival of

1801, the largest and most dramatic revival in the history of the opening of the West.

When Daniel Boone first explored Kentucky in the 1760s he came across a stretch of some fifteen miles of tall cane, some of it large enough to make fishing poles. It was a beautiful spot, fertile and open, and Daniel Boone recommended it to the settlers who poured across the mountains and through the Cumberland Gap after the American Revolution.

Most of the families that settled at Cane Ridge were Scotch-Irish Presbyterians who had been together in the Isles, came to the New World, and settled in Pennsylvania. Then they or their children moved to Virginia and North Carolina, and into the wilderness of Kentucky.

One of the first things they did at Cane Ridge was build a Presbyterian meetinghouse, which to this day remains one of the largest log buildings of the New World. It was built in 1791, mostly of blue ash cut from the nearby forest. The white settlers sat on benches, while the black slaves sat in the gallery they reached by a ladder from the outside.

The revival at Cane Ridge was in August 1801 and lasted six days and nights. As many as twenty-five thousand pioneer settlers, some from as far away as one hundred miles, came to Cane Ridge to pray, to take communion, and to see what was going on. The log meetinghouse could only hold one hundred souls at a time so preaching stands were set up outside. The Presbyterians were on one side of the meetinghouse, the Methodists on another, and the Baptists scattered around.

The greatest excitement, and what was watched most closely, were the people who during the course of the preaching fainted, swooned, went into comas, jerked, barked, laughed, or spoke in tongues. It was said they were "slain." The estimate of people slain during the six day revival was one thousand.

One of the many ministers attending the revival wrote home of this event:

"Sinners dropping down on every hand, shrieking,

131

groaning, crying for mercy, convoluted; professors [of religion] praying, agonizing, fainting, falling down in distress, for sinners, or in raptures of joy! Some singing, some shouting, clapping their hands, hugging and even kissing, laughing; others talking to the distressed, to one another, or to opposers of the work, and all this at once – no spectacle can excite a stronger sensation. And with what is doing, the darkness of the night, the solemnity of the place, and of the occasion, and conscious guilt, all conspire to make terror thrill through every power of the soul, and rouse it to awful attention."

It was at Cane Ridge that the coming of the Millennium was preached to the largest revival in the history of the New World, and it was there that Representative Stan Lee's Christian Church was founded. Meeting Representative Lee was a direct greeting from the Second Awakening.

Pat and I hastily fled from the solemn declarations of a very serious man, who seemed to walk the path from Cane Ridge of the 1800s frontier revival to his office in the capitol building in Frankfort. When you stopped being amazed, it was scary. Our common motive was to just get the hell away from there, and we did.

Representative Stan Lee and his reliance on scripture and devotion to God was not a singular event in my experiences in the Kentucky Legislature.

During the 2001 legislative session I came to know about Brother Joe Adams. Brother Joe was the often-present, ever- smiling, and willing witness to Kentucky legislators' devotion to the gospel of Jesus Christ.

Brother Joe Adams was "Chaplain to Kentucky State Government, and Washington, D.C." That is what his card and his literature said.

Brother Joe, by his own description, was a right-wing, conservative fundamentalist, who realized at age seven he was a sinner, found Christ at age ten, and began preaching at fourteen. He believed in the inerrancy of the King James Bible, and he believed that the scriptures provided all the facts and all the truths necessary to answer questions of life on earth, and thereafter.

Brother Joe was a loquacious man, and while there was never any doubt in what he believed and where he stood, he had no sharp edges. He was much given to preaching and would say very solemnly that anyone who did not accept the Bible as literal fact and accept Jesus as the savior would go to eternal hell. If a listener was offended, Brother Joe would pause and give assurances he didn't mean it personally. He was prone to say, "Only if the shoe fits..." Brother Joe smiled with a real, somewhat shy, smile.

When Brother Joe said there is only one truth and it is the Bible and all else is false, he said it without reservation and beyond debate. The implication that anyone who didn't believe this was an idiot didn't come through. It had to be there logically, but you didn't sense it from the way Brother Joe talked.

We often saw Brother Joe in the capitol leading groups of young people on tours. He took them to the supreme court chambers, the House of Representatives, the Senate, and the capitol rotunda where the statues of Abraham Lincoln, Henry Clay, Alben Barkley, Ephraim McDowell, and Jeff Davis stood tall. Brother Joe taught the young people about government and about God.

We were told Brother Joe used to frequent the floor of the House of Representatives, with floor privileges granted by the Speaker. When that anomaly was questioned by Representative Kathy Stein, Brother Joe withdrew. He later invited Kathy to come to one of his church services, and she attended.

Brother Joe's ministry to government started over twenty years ago while he was minister at the Bloomfield Baptist Church. He took his trailer to the lake one weekend for a retreat and God told Brother Joe it was his mission to minister to those doing God's work in the legislature. Brother Joe gave up his church (and its salary) and went to the capitol in Frankfort.

Brother Joe bought an old bookmobile and converted it into an office and a place to sleep. He parked it on a side street in Frankfort and that was where he lived. The legislative session started in the wintertime and the bookmobile didn't have any heat, but Brother Joe persevered.

He started first with prayer breakfasts in the basement cafeteria of the annex and before long a number of legislators were attending in the hour before the eight o'clock committee meetings began. And then Brother Joe made himself available to individual legislators to counsel and to pray, or whatever their need might be. As the years passed Brother Joe became an institution. Several times over the years the legislature passed resolutions commending Brother Joe for his work and he would thank them. Each time someone suggested he be paid for his services, Brother Joe said, "No, I work only for the Lord."

Part of Brother Joe's work for the Lord was to pass out copies of the New Testament to each member at each legislative session. He raised the money for the printing, and each copy was marked to show the reader those sections Brother Joe thought most important for salvation.

Brother Joe also published a newsletter for the legislators with his views on the wishes of the Lord on pending legislation. The Lord was opposed to abortion; was for home and religious schooling without government regulation; was against homo-sexuality; and favored the death penalty.

When I saw Brother Joe he spoke to me very kindly, and his parting words were:

"You show me one place in the Bible where it says we should not execute murderers, and I'll be with you. If we don't have executions, we don't respect life."

• • • •

Our continual volunteer activity made the thirty-day session go by quickly. At the end we counted a total of over one hundred persons who had come on a Tuesday, Wednesday, or Thursday of each week of the session. Shepherding them had been a full-time and interesting task. The overall effect was terrific.

We had become anything but a fringe group. They knew we were there, and from meeting and talking to our volunteers the legislators knew we weren't going away. Our volunteers, whether they were religiously motivated or not, were solid, serious, and dedicated citizens whose only interest was making Kentucky a less violent and more civilized home for everyone.

During the session our volunteers obtained new solid commitments for the juvenile bill from ten representatives and two senators, and for the abolition bill, four representatives and one senator.

There were few significant bills of any kind passed in this first odd-year short session, and certainly nothing controversial, but it gave us an opportunity to continue our drumbeat and to prepare for the next major session in 2002.

In the concluding week of the 2001 session Jane Chiles, executive director of the Catholic Conference, met with Gross Lindsay on Catholic Conference matters, and at the end of the meeting Representative Lindsay said to Jane, "I'm going to give you people an opportunity for a full hearing on death penalty issues. I'm scheduling two hours, the whole session, for the joint interim meeting of the Judiciary Committees in October."

Jane was surprised and delighted, and said we'd be there.

When Jane reported to the rest of us we also were delighted, but we wondered what in the world was going on. What had happened to make him do that? We didn't know.

During the interim, between regular meetings of the legislature, the standing committees of the House and Senate continue to meet and discuss proposed legislation, citizens' concerns, and general problems. These committees, which included the Judiciary Committee, meet jointly so the committee members from both the House and the Senate are in attendance. The scheduled date for the joint interim meeting of the House and Senate Judiciary Committee for the fall was October 16.

Not long after Gross Lindsay's announcement to Jane, Pat and I were visitors at a meeting of the Kentucky Criminal Justice

Council—an advisory board to the legislature chaired by the Secretary of the Justice Cabinet. Their published agenda included consideration of conducting a study of the death penalty in Kentucky. Of course, we were curious. I heard the suggestion for the study came from several members of the council, including the chair, who had read *The Second Grave*. I was pleased with this connection, but as I watched and listened it became clear that nothing was ever likely to happen in this group, and my ego settled down.

The significance of this meeting, however, was that Representative Lindsay showed up. He was not a member of the council but he had been invited to comment on some issues that were of concern to the council. This was an opportunity Pat and I hadn't anticipated, and we passed Gross Lindsay a note asking if we could meet briefly when he was finished.

Sure enough, he signaled he was agreeable and the three of us met in the foyer outside the meeting room.

"Representative Lindsay, we thank you for the opportunity of a hearing. Is there any particular aspect or bills the committee wants us to cover?"

"No, not at all," he replied. "You can do anything you want to. You have an hour and you use it however you wish. You know as well as I do, the Judiciary Committee has a very heavy docket during the session, and if we can conduct hearings in the interim then the committee has all that information and it saves us time during the session."

"Okay," we said, "we'll see you in October."

"All right," he replied, and went out the door.

Pat and I had no idea what was really going on. Did Gross Lindsay feel bad because he had cut us short in the hearing in 2000? Was he impressed with our volunteers during the short session? Was he playing games with us? We didn't know.

The truth was we were elated and anxious to put together our presentation, and perfectly willing to take Gross Lindsay at his word. He was having the hearing on abolishing the death penalty in the interim to save time in the regular session. We assumed that meant our abolition bills could be posted in committee for a vote without the necessity of another time-consuming hearing. We would put on our case in the October interim committee meeting, and be ready for posting and a vote in the 2002 session. That was the logical conclusion from what we were told.

It was just April, so we had plenty of time to plan our presentation. We began an internal debate on the most effective approach, and what witnesses would command the most attention.

We so carefully planned the hearing for the 2000 session, and it was such a bust, I wasn't sure where to start with planning this next one. We talked about it, and one suggestion was to bring the committee the experiences of one of the twelve states that did not have the death penalty. How did they get along without executions? That sounded good to me.

The most obvious choice would be our neighbor, West Virginia, just across the mountains. The death penalty had been part of the culture and the law of West Virginia from the earliest days until 1965 when it so happened that the governor and a handful of leaders in the West Virginia legislature opposed the death penalty and managed to get an abolition bill into law.

Most people in Kentucky think of West Virginia as a more violent state than Kentucky; but the facts are West Virginia has no death penalty and their homicide rate is half ours. We decided to search for someone who would be a witness from West Virginia.

Through ACLU circles I had met a very pleasant and thoughtful man named Chuck Smith, a professor of political science at a West Virginia College. I found his telephone number and called to ask whom I might possibly get to come and testify about how West Virginia got along without the death penalty.

Chuck was glad to help. He understood we wanted someone of stature, who was knowledgeable, and willing to help. He gave me some names of possibilities, judges and public figures, and talked and wrote to a number of people himself. The search for the ideal West Virginian who would come to Kentucky and take on our Judiciary Committees continued almost right up to the time of the hearing.

We decided not to repeat what we did in 2000. The one person who had really gotten on in 2000 was Representative Bob Heleringer. He'd had had his day, and his say, and he wanted nothing more. Kenyon Meyer and Father Dick Sullivan did at least a truncated version of the Frank Tamme case, but now we had the great decision from the Fayette Circuit Court granting Frank Tamme a new trial. That decision had been appealed by the prosecution to the Kentucky Supreme Court. We did not want to do anything that might prejudice Frank Tamme's case, so we decided to leave it alone. We would start fresh.

One of the witnesses we had not been able to present in 2000 was Paul Stevens, representing murder victims' families opposed to the death penalty. We thought we should ask him again. His message was not only persuasive and powerful, he also took much of the steam out of the case for the victims' families who opposed us.

We also thought it would be helpful to remind the committee of the history and development of the abolition campaign, how the movement had grown and with it the favorable changes in public opinion regarding the death penalty. This would be my assignment. Then we would have the witness from West Virginia, and probably finish up with Jane Chiles.

The general outline of our presentation began to take shape, and we agreed (once again) to share the time with the proponents of the juvenile bill. The advocates of the juvenile bill said they intended to call once again Dr. Ralph Kelly, Dr. Kerby Neill, and Shelia Schuster, and that was fine.

That was about it, and I began to run out of steam. Enough of death, politics, and religion for a while. My wife Stephanie and I needed an ocean fix, and we had a marvelous one at Cape May.

11

THE CASTLE

Paul Stevens mentioned more than once that he wanted me to meet Sister Chris Beckett who worked with him as a volunteer chaplain at the Kentucky State Penitentiary at Eddyville. Paul said, simply, "I think you two would like each other."

As it happened, I was invited to give a talk to a Catholic group in Owensboro, and Sister Chris was there and we met.

I guess Sister Chris (or just Chris, as many called her) was in her mid to late forties. She was short and somewhat stocky and her persona was much defined by her eyes. She had a joyous smile and laugh, but whether her demeanor was happy or serious, her eyes dominated. They grew very dark when she was angry and lit up like candles when she was delighted. They were wide apart in a pleasant round face on each side of a button nose. Sister Chris was president of the Glenmary Order in Western Kentucky, and Paul Stevens was right, we did hit it off pretty well.

After my talk at the civic center we had coffee and I asked about her and her Order. She looked at me and said, "If you want to see what I do you should come to Eddyville and go with me while I make my rounds at the penitentiary."

"Could I do that?" I asked.

"It shouldn't be difficult getting you into the prison general population, but they won't let much of anyone on death row. Do you want to try? I will write the warden and we'll see what he says."

"Sure," I said, and I wrote down my date of birth and social security number, which she said she would need. "See if you can get me on death row. Tell the warden I've written a book, and may write another one."

Sister Chris seemed excited at the idea of me joining her on her Thursday visit to the penitentiary, and said she would see what she could do.

Within the week she e-mailed me a copy of the letter she sent the warden and within a week or so of that she called and said laughing, "They're not only going to let you in, the warden says you can go on death row with me. How about that!"

I was surprised and pleased that I was going to see the inside of the Kentucky State Penitentiary, which was often called "the Castle." I don't know who first named it that, but they got it right.

The Kentucky State Penitentiary sits on a rise just outside the small city of Eddyville and directly on the banks of an enormous lake created by damming the Cumberland River, and named after the Vice President and Kentucky Senator Alben Barkley. Lake Barkley, and its twin to the east, Kentucky Lake, provided Western Kentucky and much of the central United States with exceptionally wild and beautiful sites for fishing and camping.

Peering over it all from the heights was this enormous stone bulk. It had turrets, deep slit windows in the stone, and the heavy solemnity of permanence. It did look like a castle.

The road from town wound unevenly around small farms and came upon the penitentiary from the rear. It was first visible after a bend at the top of a rise. It was a sprawling complex with a twelve-foot-high double chainlink fence topped with coils of silver barbed wire curling and catching the light, dancing around the border of the acres of the compound.

I approached slowly, my eyes caught by the coils of wire glistening in the sun, interrupted occasionally by buildings set along the perimeter. I saw the Castle itself at the top of the rise facing east. I stopped on the side of the road and gazed at the stone fortress. It stood in heavy contrast to the white caps visibly flickering in the winds on Lake Barkley below. Appended to the sides of the Castle were brick additions built through the years.

Parking was not easy and as I looked for a space along the road I noticed, just across from the penitentiary, a small white house with a side yard and a white picket fence. Facing the penitentiary in the yard of the little house was a statue of Jesus, hands outstretched, reaching toward the dark barred slits in the side of the Castle. Surrounding Jesus throughout the yard were smaller statutes that I assumed were figures of the Apostles.

I sat in my car between the Castle, the lake, and the icons, feeling unsettled. I was surrounded by views that in other contexts would not be unfamiliar, but here and now appeared very strange.

I followed the road almost down to the lake and finally found a place for my car. After parking I started the long trudge back up the hill to the penitentiary entrance.

Sister Chris asked me to meet her at the entrance security station at 10:00 a.m. and I was a few minutes early so I took my time on the long climb. I was looking forward to seeing her. During this visit, and a number of others during the campaign, I came to know some of the story of her life.

She was, she told me, "a cradle Catholic. Both my mom and my dad were Catholic. She was Irish and he was German." The most impressive things in her early life, Chris said, were the fierce force of her mother's passion for children and social reform, her grandmother's love of her Catholic faith, and the German tradition of discipline and education.

Her teenage and college years were the times of the Vietnam War, the Civil Rights Movement, the assassinations of John and Bobby Kennedy, and Martin Luther King, Jr. and Malcolm X, and the Council and changes of Vatican II, all of which influenced her views of society, faith, and of herself. Like her mother, she took the plight of the poor and oppressed seriously, and like her grandmother, she embraced the Catholic faith with a full love.

These passions led her, she says in retrospect, "almost inevitably" to a religious life. She began the journey as a volunteer in the integrating of the schools in the south and a year later entered the Glenmary Sisters.

Religious life and ministry offered Sister Chris opportunities in both education and service. She was first sent to Georgia in the early seventies to work in setting up the first local integrated day care center for the poor. She taught and organized voter registration of blacks and refused to be intimidated by the Ku Klux Klan. She was often frightened, but she loved the work. Later, Sister Chris attended St. Louis University where she received a bachelor's degree in English, and later a master's degree in Spiritual Theology.

Sister Chris' first introduction to Kentucky was helping to open a new mission covering six rural and mountainous Eastern Kentucky counties. They organized volunteer college students who called themselves" Turtles" and often traveled with Chris to visit and work with mountain people of the ridges and hollows. She said, "When I first came here and worked in the mountains, those were good years. I think it was then I became a real person— walking the walk. I'll tell you it was wild. One family I got to know—Fred and Bethel—they had five kids and five pigs and lived in the worst shack you ever saw in your life. Well, Fred and Bethel managed to get a trailer, not a doublewide, but still a good house trailer. When they got it all set up it looked like the Ritz next to their shack. Well, Fred and Bethel moved in with the five kids, and then the five pigs. It wasn't long before the trailer didn't look a whole lot better than the old shack."

Chris would laugh telling her stories, her eyes moist.

Sister Chris moved to Kentucky to stay when the headquarters of the Glenmary Sisters was moved to the western Kentucky town of Owensboro, not too far from the penitentiary at Eddyville. Reading Sister Helen Prejean's *Dead Man Walking*, and meeting Paul Stevens, led her to her mission as volunteer chaplain at the Kentucky State Penitentiary.

After climbing the hill from the lakeshore I was greeted by stone steps up three more levels. I finally reached the penitentiary entrance, and paused at the massive doors. I knew I'd done some climbing. The front vestibule was small. There was a guard sitting behind a table to the left, a walk-through metal detector in the middle, and then heavy gray bars from floor to ceiling, centered with a ponderous door.

I was showing the guard my driver's license when I heard a musical chuckle from behind the bars and Sister Chris' voice, "Well, there he is, he made it up the hill." I greeted her as best I could through all the bars. After I signed in, emptied my pockets, was patted and screened, I was permitted through the prison door and greeted by Sister Chris with a hug. She knew the guards by name and she introduced me to them one by one, like I was meeting her friends in a coffee shop. I said polite hellos. No one offered a hand, and I kept mine by my side.

Sister Chris asked, "Are you ready?" I nodded and we headed toward the central prison yard. The first barrier was six feet away, another wall of steel bars, and another ponderous door. We stood facing it. Sister Chris started fidgeting but we waited until there was a buzz of the lock releasing. Sister Chris pushed the heavy door open and we entered a concrete corridor. At the end of the corridor was another wall of gray bars, another locked door. Apparently someone we couldn't see was watching us and after another spell of waiting there was another buzz and this time I opened the door and we proceeded through the labyrinth. In all there were five doors to be opened and closed from the foyer to the yard, and what I remembered most vividly was the deep heavy sound of each door as it clanged shut and locked behind us. I sought some reassurance in my mind against the note of finality in each of those jarring noises, and all I found was uneasiness.

The open yard brought the relief of sunlight. It looked very much like the open courtyard of a real castle. The first things that struck me were the contrasting colors. A dazzling clear blue sky, startling relief from gray steel and concrete, and immaculately clean khaki brown uniforms and white undershirts worn by the several dozen men in the yard.

These men, Chris told me, were G.P.s, the prisoners designated as "general population." They were all felons, murderers, or whatever, milling around during their free time, staring off into space or in quiet conversation.

As we walked I could see men maneuvering to get close, trying not to be too obvious, but wanting to speak to Sister Chris, sometimes with a small smile, most often with a frown of concentration.

"Did you get hold of Martha?"

"Yes," Chris responded, "she says things are getting better."

"Did you tell her I was trying to reach her?"

"Yes, John, I did. I think it's going to be okay."

"Thanks, Chris."

A young skinny kid: "Chris, I heard from my lawyer. She says our case is really looking up." He hugged Chris and she looked up at him. "That's very good, Mike. Remember, just believe."

A man who looked like a prize fighter, with a burr haircut, pushed the others aside to get close to Chris, and said: "Have you heard what happened? You won't believe this," and the rest he spoke animatedly, but close to Chris' ear so no one else could hear. Chris listened very seriously with no hint of approval or disapproval.

So it went the length of the yard. Many of the men ignored us completely, but for those who came up, Sister Chris was a link to the outside, a friend, a source of nonjudgmental help and advice.

She took it all very slowly and carefully, often with a hug. If she felt impatient she didn't let it show. Every conversation she ended with something upbeat. "We'll see. It will be okay. Give it a chance." And often, "Just believe."

At the end of the concrete walk along the side of the yard was another barred door. Chris had a walkie-talkie she took from her belt and she said into it that she was at gate six with an authorized visitor and wished to enter. We waited there staring at the door. I could not tell where the guard was who could see us but shortly there was the buzz and we could open the door.

"Now," Chris said, as we made our way down another concrete and barred corridor, "Are you ready for death row?"

I had no idea if I was ready. I was anxious to see what it was like. I was self-conscious and worried I would look like someone peering at animals in a zoo. I really didn't know quite what to feel.

At the end of the corridor we arrived at another barred door and I could see through to a glass-enclosed guard station on a raised platform. The two guards in it were looking down at us. Neither was smiling. In all my memories of my visit to the penitentiary, there are only a few of seeing a smile.

Sister Chris talked to the guards on her walkie-talkie and explained at length who I was and told them they should have a copy of the warden's approval of my visit. There was a pause and they said they did not have a copy. This was followed by a wait and obviously calls being made back and forth to the front security office and the warden's office. I stood there, Sister Chris fidgeted, and ultimately the buzzer sounded and we entered death row.

It was quiet, and very clean. There were bars around every open space. The cells were to our left as we entered and continued around three sides of a quadrant. Each cell was about seven feet wide and fourteen feet deep, with a narrow barred window at the end, a cot, basin, toilet, chair and desk, and a small bookcase. That was what was issued. Death row was the sections of these cells on the first of the three floors, with a space in the middle containing a few pieces of exercise equipment and surrounding bars.

The sense of cleanliness was because the concrete and steel were scrubbed down twice a day, every day. It was quiet because the hubbub of the yard was shut out, and the men on death row did not have all that much to say.

The men were either in their cells or doing a chore on the row. No one was in the exercise area at the time but the men were permitted to exercise, a third of them at a time, for an hour every day. Their every movement could be observed by the guards situated above. Death row impressed me as a desperately lonely place. Sister Chris took a deep breath, reached over and touched my arm, and the two of us headed to the first cell on the row.

I was curious and though I felt uneasy looking into the cell, of course I did. There was a slender, middle-aged man sitting on a cot against the back wall of the cubicle. He looked at us and came forward and greeted Sister Chris.

"Hi, Chris, what'd'ya know?" was his greeting.

"Hello Tom, I'm fine. How's it going with you?"

They could have been meeting at the intersection of Third and Main anywhere, but they weren't, and they both knew it. I watched and took all this in. It occurred to me that it helped to treat the extraordinary as ordinary. For a man waiting to be killed, it helped not to be reminded.

Sister Chris looked toward me and said, "Tom, this is the man who wrote the book, *The Second Grave*."

Tom looked at me. "No kidding. Well, what do you know? That's some book. I've still got it over there somewhere. I'm real glad to meet you," and his arm came sliding through the bars and we shook hands.

We proceeded down the row. Some of the men gave no recognition to our passing, one or two looked up and nodded, but many of the men on death row appeared pleased to see Sister Chris and responded pleasantly to her introduction of "the man who wrote the book."

I had researched the stories of many of these men on death row, but the strangeness and the emotion of actually being there made it difficult for me to put the face and the name and the story together. It was just a line of human beings in cages, each in a terrible plight.

When a prisoner came forward to greet Chris she stopped and reached out to shake his hand. After introducing me, she talked to the man easily and earnestly, and listened the same way. She smiled and praised the good news, and expressed regret and concern for the bad.

Sister Chris knew the Catholic men on death row who liked to take Communion when she was there. When we reached the first of these, after the introductions and the talk, she asked if he would like Communion. He nodded yes. Sister Chris reached into her bag and brought out a small container of wafers she held under her arm while she and the prisoner held hands and said the Lord's Prayer. Then she took a wafer and reaching through the bars placed it on the man's tongue, saying, "The body of Christ." The prisoner chewed quietly, and murmured a solemn, "Amen."

I stood back a few paces, my hands together in front of me, watching quietly.

The second man Chris asked about Communion was a tall black man and after he reached his arms through the bars Chris looked at me and said, "Will you join hands with us?" I moved next to her and took the prisoner's hand and Sister Chris' hand in my hands and the three of us were joined as we said the Lord's Prayer. We each had our head bowed, and my gaze was directly on the prisoner's hand clasping mine. The contrast between his long black gracefully tapered fingers and my scrawny old white ones was dramatic. I admired the beauty of his hands and I wondered what unthinkable violence they had done.

The major occupation on death row was finding something to do. It was ironic that these men, struggling so hard and thinking so much about avoiding execution and staying alive, had so little to occupy the time they were winning. Some worked at reading law books and hand-writing motions, petitions, and briefs to be mailed to some court seeking relief and release. Others did odd bits of this and that, establishing specific daily routines. But for most there was nothing to do.

Each of the men were assigned duties: doing the wash, scrubbing or sweeping the floors, delivering meals, anything that could be thought up that would pass time and give the appearance at least of something being accomplished.

Within their cells the men could wear anything they wanted that was clean and decent. Once they stepped outside their cell they were required to wear red pants and red shirts. The general prison population wore khaki; the men on death row wore red. Each man wore an identification badge with his picture on a chain around his neck.

One thing about the men on death row, even those with obvious mental problems—they were all polite. There was no hollering or banging or carrying on, at least while I was there. As we continued on Chris' rounds I watched each pale face as it appeared at the cell front. Even the blacks seemed pale to me. Listening to the questions and requests I felt the deep struggle in these men to discover some sense of worth, some purpose, any indication that life on death row had some meaning. This was not easy.

Finally, at the end of the cellblocks, and after the last goodbye, Chris and I stood there looking back over the scene. It occurred to me we had not seen Frank Tamme, and I asked Chris about him. She paused, putting a finger to her cheek. "That's right. I don't know. I'll ask. Maybe he's back in the hospital."

After the usual wait the heavy door opened and we walked out. The bright light of the courtyard and the free movement of the general population men on break were a relief to both the eye and the heart. I was glad I saw death row. I was also glad it was over. I did not want to go back.

During her talks with the men in general population Chris asked if they'd be coming to chapel for noon services. That is where she now took me. There was a door to the chapel off the courtyard and we entered into a plain room with a pulpit at one end and folding chairs against the wall. She led me through it to another room with small offices that were used by the volunteer chaplains and for private meetings with prisoners.

Chris introduced me to a Catholic priest sitting behind a small desk and to a retired Baptist minister he had been talking to. We didn't have much to say to each other after the introductions so I followed Chris as she was milling with the men who were coming in.

At one point she stopped, took my arm, and led me to a

corner where we could talk. She said: "I think there are going to be two men in here in a minute I want you to talk to. One's called Leo, and the other Snake. They've been in prison for a long time and they used to be real troublemakers here. Both of them got sent away to other institutions in a program they have of moving trouble makers around, but they both were brought back here a couple of years ago at about the same time.

"They met in the courtyard not long after they got back and got to talking, and decided they had had enough of trouble-making, they wanted to do something else. They started trying to figure out what they could do and they hit on the idea of recycling pop cans. That's right," Chris looked at me laughing, "the prison was putting all the pop cans in with the garbage and sending them off to the dump. Leo and Snake brought the idea to me of separating out the cans and selling them to recycle and using the money to start a charity for kids in the local communities.

"I said, 'Wow, why not?" and helped them write a letter to the warden asking for permission. After awhile, he agreed. When they come in I will introduce you and they can tell you all about it."

It wasn't long before two men came in and headed for Sister Chris, and, of course, I knew it must be Leo and Snake. One of them, and I think it was Leo, was bearded, and both of them looked like old hands at prison life.

Without any hesitation they told me about their project. It was now beginning its second year and the receipts for the first year were over five thousand dollars. Most of it went to a child in Hopkinsville suffering from leukemia. They showed me the little girl's picture.

The two men took turns telling me the details—of how they had convinced the warden; of the system that had been established for separating and collecting cans at various locations in the compound; of their experiences with the buyers; and, how they selected the kids to receive help. It was clear they had become businessmen running a thriving business at the Kentucky State Penitentiary.

At one point I asked, "What in the world made you decide to do this? What happened?"

They looked at each other and then at the ground and neither responded until Snake looked up and said to me, "You ever spend time in the hole?"

I shook my head.

"Leo and I have both spent a lot of time in the hole. You're in solitary and no windows or nothing but a metal slide where the meals come in.

"If you spend enough time in the hole you get to thinking. Sooner or later you realize there has got to be some better ways to do things. You can't spend too much time in the hole. It'll get to you.

"Leo and I decided we'd had enough of the hole. So now we run a business to help kids."

I shook hands with Leo and Snake and returned to Sister Chris.

The men assembled for services and as the room filled a guy headed toward me carrying a folder full of papers.

"You Carl?" he asked, and I nodded. "Chris told me about you and said you're a writer." I nodded again and he said, "Me too," and he opened his folder.

He introduced himself as Joe Knight and what he wanted to show me was a pile of poems. We sat down at a small table and he told me about his poems, describing each one as he handed me a typed paper. There was one called "Incarceration," one called "Marked Men," and so on.

I listened and skimmed each poem as he handed it to me and said polite things with interest and encouragement. Nothing came across very well to me, and I suppose they were pretty much what you would expect, given the circumstances, but then he handed me this very short poem:

A VIEW OUTSIDE MY WINDOW

I gaze out the chicken mesh windowpane.
The golden light of another glaring dawn
breaks into burning stars
when it hits the rolled razor wire
set against the azure sky,
smudged with pink and purple hues.
Shifting clouds of pearl cast shadows
on the silver water tower, KSP
for the Kentucky State Penitentiary
lettered in flat black paint on the luminous globe.

12

THE 2001 INTERIM HEARING

The October 16 hearing with the House and Senate Judiciary Committees was getting closer. Our materials and witnesses were almost ready except for our witness from West Virginia. We thought we had a highly respected appellate judge from Charlestown, but he decided he couldn't for reasons that were not too clear. We were still empty-handed.

I thought surely we could find someone. More and more I was on the phone with possibilities suggested by Chuck Smith, and then with possibilities suggested by possibilities.

Along the way a professor who turned us down said, "You know who would be ideal for you is Senator Bill Wooton. He is a good man, strongly opposes the death penalty and is chair of the Judiciary Committee in the West Virginia senate. I suspect he would be willing to do it if he can."

Senator William R. Wooton was a practicing attorney and I found him at his office in Beckley, West Virginia. When I explained what I needed we talked for a few minutes about West Virginia's abolition of the death penalty. His conversation was thoughtful and his voice mild.

"Can you possibly come to Kentucky for our hearing in Frankfort on October 16 and testify about the West Virginia experience?"

"Well, let me see. I'll get my calendar," and there was a pause while I assumed he was rummaging around looking for his schedule book.

"Here we are—you say Tuesday, October 16—No, I've got

a meeting scheduled in Charleston on that day. I'm sorry"—and he paused and I waited. After a moment Senator Wooton said, "Can you and I agree that you asked me to do this some time ago, and I committed that I'd be there?"

"Sure," I said.

"It would be nice to have an excuse not to have to go to that meeting in Charleston, and you're my excuse. I will be in Frankfort, Kentucky, on the sixteenth of October."

"That's great. I'll send you some stuff on our campaign and the hearing, and you and I will get together sometime before the hearing and talk over your testimony. We all thank you very much, and look forward to meeting you." That was it. We were set, and I was most pleased with our luck in getting Senator Bill Wooton.

I met him the evening before the hearing at his hotel to discuss his testimony. I have a stereotype in my head, I'm not sure why, of politicians as garrulous, outgoing personalities. It invariably surprises me when I meet (as I sometimes do) mild mannered, introspective, quiet, and shy politicians. There are plenty of them, and Senator Wooton was one.

We talked for a while about our situation in Kentucky and the strong public approval in the state for the death penalty. He understood the point I wanted to make with his presence was that a politician could be an abolitionist and survive.

We talked about West Virginia and how they managed to keep the death penalty from being reinstated. Senator Wooton brought stacks of statistics on the homicide rates in West Virginia, which were much lower than those in Kentucky. I did what I could to encourage him to put some oomph in his presentation. He understood and said he'd do the best he could.

We were ready to go.

Hearing room 149 on the first floor of the annex began to fill by 9:30 and we were due to start at 10:00. Our press releases were out, written materials prepared and distributed, and I was wearing my "go to court" suit and tie. I swore when I retired that

I wouldn't put that stuff on again, but of course I had to.

We were all nervous and fidgety but pleased as our supporters, each wearing the blue and white sticker, filled the room and began to overflow into the adjacent auxiliary room. Press, radio, and TV people were also piling in, so we would be well covered.

The two chairmen, Robert Stivers of the Senate and Gross Lindsay of the House of Representatives, were both there. They alternated serving as chair in the interim meetings, and this meeting was Representative Lindsay's turn. At about 10:10 he gaveled the hearing to order and the secretary called the roll.

The Joint Committee has twenty-eight members from the House and the Senate, and twenty-two showed up. They didn't all stay throughout the hearing but there was not much I could do about that, other than take note.

This was quite a sight. Twenty-two Senators and Representatives, many of the faces now familiar, sitting behind the continuous desks on the two semicircular tiers, looking down on us like Roman senators gazing upon the multitudes.

After Representative Lindsay acknowledged a quorum he squinted, looking at us over his glasses, and began his customary announcement when there was a full house and a contested issue.

"Now, I'll say to all of you, in the interest of decorum, there will be no cheering or clapping, or things of that nature. It just interrupts the meeting. The only thing on our agenda today is the death penalty, and each side will get one hour, and committee members will have an opportunity to ask questions. The opponents of the death penalty will go first," and looking down at us, "Who is going to lead off, Reverend Delahanty, or Mr. Wedekind?"

"I will start off, Mr. Chairman," I replied, since it was my job to outline the proceedings, define the issues, and make the introductions. I took a seat at the witness table and looked up at all of them.

"Thank you, Mr. Chairman and ladies and gentlemen of the committees. You each have in front of you a document we

154

have prepared for the hearing which, if you'll take a look, sets forth the issues on page two, and on the succeeding six pages presents the salient facts on these issues."

I touched briefly on the contents of each of these pages, and I could see most of them following along with me.

"We will present to you individuals who are knowledgeable about and have had intimate connections with the death penalty, and we will start with the testimony of Mr. Paul Stevens. Please come forward, Mr. Stevens."

I said no more than that about Paul Stevens because he now had time to fully tell his story himself. He came to the witness table in his deliberate manner, took a seat, and slowly began.

I watched the faces and the attention span of the committee members as Paul related the horrors of the murder of his daughter, Cindy.

"The phone rang at 3 a.m. and a voice said, 'There is something wrong with Cindy.'" Then he had found her murdered.

The saga of his life after that, and ultimately joining the campaign to abolish the death penalty, was told matter of factly. Paul's manner was such no one could doubt his honesty or sincerity.

When he was finished he sat in his seat and looked at the members of the committee. I had asked the chair to hold committee questions until our witnesses had finished, but even so I cannot imagine anyone on the committee daring to ask any questions of Paul.

"Next, Mr. Chairman, Father Pat Delahanty will speak to you on the special issue of executing the mentally retarded."

Pat came forward and took the seat and placed in front of him a copy of his statement, which he had handwritten.

Kentucky had passed an act in 1990, mainly due to Pat's efforts, prohibiting the execution of the mentally retarded. At that time the Department of Corrections certified there was no one then on death row that was mentally retarded, so the 1990 act was prospective only.

It turned out the department was wrong. There were at least two people on death row that we believed could meet the criteria of mental retardation. Their attorneys wanted the right to present that evidence to a court. Pat made a strong pitch for the committee to approve a bill authorizing them to do so, by making the 1990 act applicable to those then on death row.

He said it well, he said it succinctly, and when he was finished reading his statement he looked at the committee with an attitude of, "How could you not?"

When preparing for the hearing we decided to intermix our witnesses for abolition with the witnesses for the juvenile bill. The next three witnesses were on the juvenile bill.

The first was Shelia Schuster, the director of Professional Affairs for the Kentucky Psychological Association. She testified that the United States was isolated in the world in killing children, with our only compatriots being Iraq, Pakistan, Nigeria, Saudi Arabia, the Congo, and Yemen. She concluded her remarks by reminding the committee that recent polls showed almost 80 percent of Kentuckians opposed executing children.

Next was Dr. Ralph Kelly, commissioner of Juvenile Justice, who urged the committee to pass the juvenile bill with pretty much the same reasons he had in the earlier truncated hearing. The testimony was important because he was an official of state government, which to some gave special weight to his views.

Third was Dr. Kerby Neill, a child psychologist from Lexington, who did his usual excellent job of explaining child development in maturity and judgment, and the inappropriateness of applying the death penalty to the violent acts of sixteen and seventeen year olds. Dr. Neil had time to give some of his own background and training, and his range of experiences and accomplishments were remarkable. I thought one of the best explanations of his expertise was he and his wife had raised six children.

Next it was my time to speak, and I addressed the committee as much as was possible in that setting, in a nonconfrontational conversational manner. I spoke a bit about the history of the Kentucky Coalition to Abolish the Death Penalty and the wide range of partners now in the coalition and our significant increase in members, witness the people from all over the state filling these two large rooms on behalf of abolition.

I spoke briefly about Illinois Governor George Ryan stopping all executions because of developing evidence that many on Illinois death row were innocent or wrongfully convicted. This was not a unique situation, I pointed out. In the past twenty-five years 62 percent of all death penalty convictions in Kentucky had been set aside on appeal. There was a real risk Kentucky could execute an innocent man.

I also made the point that a person charged with murder was unlikely to end up on death row unless he was poor and couldn't afford a good lawyer, was ignorant or mentally ill, and unfortunate enough to be tried in one of our "hanging judge" counties. Seventy percent of the counties in Kentucky have never sentenced a man to death. It is the 30 percent that can get you.

Finally, I reminded the committee that there were twelve states that had abolished the death penalty in this country, including our neighboring state of West Virginia, and that we were fortunate to have as our next witness a distinguished attorney and senator from West Virginia, chair of the West Virginia's Senate Judiciary Committee, the Honorable William R. Wooton.

I thought perhaps Gross Lindsay, as chair of the Joint Judiciary Committee of Kentucky, might make some special greeting or courtesy to a fellow politician and chair from a neighboring state, but he did not.

Senator Wooton took his seat and thanked the committee for the opportunity to speak to them.

"Let me assure you," he commenced, "I am not here in any manner or form to try and tell the legislature of Kentucky what it should do. That is not any of my business, I assure you. I know you are quite capable of handling your own affairs.

"I will, however, give you some background on what we

have done in West Virginia, and how it is working. If that is of any use to you in your deliberations that will be fine."

Bill Wooton said all of this very seriously in his quiet voice, and I thought it sat well with the committee.

He described how West Virginia abolished the death penalty in 1965, before he was in the legislature, and that their criminal justice system worked well without it. West Virginia's historically low homicide rate remained low. It was his judgment, he said, that his state was much better off without executions.

Because he knew he was not an orator, Senator Wooton brought with him a copy of a speech against the death penalty that he admired and he read excerpts to the committee.

It was about as low key as you could get but I hoped his appearance had an effect.

Our last speaker was Jane Chiles, the executive director of the Catholic Conference of Kentucky. Jane was an attractive person with a straightforward and charming way about her. Most everyone on the committee knew Jane from her past work in the legislature on Catholic issues, and they liked her whether they agreed with her or not.

Jane Chiles took her place at the table and looking up at the chairman said, "Representative Lindsay, you promised at the end of the last session that you would give us a hearing, and I personally thank you for keeping that promise, and we welcome this opportunity."

Gross Lindsay tried not to show that praise pleased him, but he was not successful.

Jane Chiles proceeded with her testimony of the position of the Catholic Conference opposing the death penalty. She recited the reasons and then paused, at first looking down at her hands folded on the table in front of her, and then finally looking up at the committee. Her face expressed strong, but controlled, emotion.

"Over the years," she started slowly, "as I have lobbied against the death penalty, a number of you have asked me, 'Jane, have you ever experienced the murder of a loved one?' If it happened to you, you would feel different.

"I pondered that question, and I had no way to know the answer. I knew what I wanted it to be, but I couldn't know what it really was.

"I have to tell you"—and here she had to catch herself and take a breath—"I now know.

"I had a most wonderful and beloved nephew, Scottie, who was the delight and love of all our family. He was bright and loving and successful, and worked on the eighty-ninth floor of the World Trade Center. Now, I have an answer to that question. I am a new member of murder victims' families."

The room froze. There was not a sound, no movement. No one had known; and the drama and horror of 9/11 flooded into each consciousness.

"My family is in deep mourning. We are changed. We want the killers to be held accountable. We recognize the terrible murders that have been committed. We know and understand the suffering of victims' families. But the question now is not what the murderers did and who they are. The question now is who we are and what we should do. I now know the answer to how I feel as one who has been dreadfully hurt. I say to you, life is in God's hands. Do not kill for me!"

Jane Chiles sat very still in the silence and I did nothing to break the spell. Gross Lindsay began shifting in his chair, and said, "All right, do you have any thing else?"

"No, Mr. Chairman," I replied, "that concludes our presentation."

"Are there questions from the committee?" Gross Lindsay looked around and called on Representative Heleringer.

Bob Heleringer, the ardent supporter of our cause, thanked Jane Chiles for being there and sharing her story. Jane was still sitting next to me at the table and she gave Bob a wan, misty-eyed smile.

"For me, this is a moral issue," he continued, "We are all sorry for what you have been through, Jane, but I agree with you that life is in God's hands and we should not be killing."

"Senator Jones," said the chair, calling on the next member with his hand raised.

Ray Jones was a handsome young lawyer from Pikeville, a new senator form Eastern Kentucky who was a conservative Democrat and no friend of abolition.

"My question, Mr. Speaker, is for Commissioner Kelly. Commissioner Kelly, you have spoken in favor of eliminating the death penalty for juveniles. Let me ask you if you have the governor's approval for this?"

"The governor's office knows I'm here, Senator."

"Does that mean the governor agrees with what you are saying?"

"I haven't talked to the governor about this. All I can tell you is I submitted my schedule and a copy of my remarks to the governor's office, and I am here."

Senator Jones seemed determined to pin down the governor's position on the Juvenile Bill, and I didn't understand why. Was he looking for a headline, "Governor opposes killing children." It made no sense to me, but that was not something new.

Several other representatives who supported our position were called on and they said agreeable things and lobbed softball questions.

The last question came from Representative Crenshaw, who was not yet with us.

"I want to ask the senator from West Virginia a question. Senator, you told us that the homicide rate in West Virginia was low, and was about half what it is in Kentucky. Can you tell me why that is?"

Senator Wooton stood up and replied, "No sir, I don't know why our rate of homicides is so low."

Jesse Crenshaw smiled in amazement at the answer, and I thought, "Honest to the end."

That was the last question from the committee for our

witnesses, and the chair said, "All right, we'll hear from speakers supporting the death penalty. Mr. Moore, I know you're here, will you come forward."

George W. Moore, commonwealth attorney for the 21st Judicial District and president of the Kentucky Commonwealth Attorney's Association, came from his seat in the audience and took my chair at the witness table. I did not know him but Pat told me he had worked with him on several issues and he thought he was an easygoing, nice guy.

"Thank you, Mr. Chairman. I am here today on behalf of the Commonwealth Attorney's Association to speak in support of the death penalty in Kentucky.

"National polls show, as this committee probably well knows, that over 60 percent of Americans support the death penalty. Now, after 9/11, that support is probably a lot higher.

"I agree, as has been said, that life is sacred, but still the public needs to be protected. The men on death row have earned their way there.

"The criminal justice system that administers the death penalty is the best in the world, and whatever we do is subject to rigorous review.

"Now the proponents of abolishing the death penalty set up straw men in their arguments. They claim the convicted did not have competent counsel. That is simply not true. Defendants in capital cases are represented by attorneys from the Department of Public Advocacy who are the best trained and most experienced attorneys in the business.

"These people cannot name for you one innocent man who has ever been executed in Kentucky. This is all a smoke screen. Not only that, these people have 'cooked the books.' They claim that death penalty prosecutions are more expensive than life in prison cases, but they don't include the costs of appeals in the life in prison cases. They are comparing apples and oranges. They stand up here and tell you the death penalty is not a deterrent to murder. That is laughable. It is common sense that a person is not going to kill if he knows that he will be killed."

That was about all he had to say. None of it was true, other than we could not prove that an innocent man had been executed.

Mr. Moore, on a more positive note, suggested to the committee that the system could be improved if they would adopt a unified system of appeals, which would basically cut down on the appeals from a death sentence and save time.

Finally, Mr. Moore warned the committee that if the juvenile bill passed, and sixteen and seventeen year-olds were not subject to the death penalty, then gangsters would hire these kids to do their killing for them, and both the grown-ups and the kids would escape the death penalty. I admit that absurdity had never occurred to me.

George Moore then introduced other commonwealth attorneys—six of them—who were in attendance and available to answer questions.

I realized then that George Moore was the only speaker in support of the death penalty. Where, I wondered, was Jo Ann Phillips and the Kentuckians Voice for Crime Victims? They were always ready to speak on the death penalty. Was it because they didn't want to go head to head with Paul Stevens, and then Jane Chiles? I had no idea, but I was glad.

"There are no more speakers, Mr. Moore?"

"No sir."

"All right, questions from committee members," and Gross Lindsay looked around at his dwindling membership and seeing a hand, said, "Representative Heleringer."

Bob Heleringer leaned forward in his chair, took off his glasses, and looking at George Moore, said:

"Mr. Moore, I want you to know I take personal offense to your remarks. You're saying the opponents of the death penalty are 'cooking the books.' That their arguments are 'amusing.' As a longtime opponent of the death penalty, I will tell you the motives and the arguments of these people are sincere. I had hoped we wouldn't get into finger pointing, but I resent what you said. It takes a lot of guts for individuals to come up here and argue an unpopular cause, and you have no business belittling them."

You could now tell from the agitation in his face and a tremor in his voice that Bob Heleringer was truly mad at what Moore had said. I personally thought it was pretty mild, but it was nice being defended. He went on.

"These people who have lost loved ones—Paul Stevens, Jane Chiles—who do not want the death penalty. It is hard for them to come up here and face that. This is a moral issue, and I resent your statements."

At the end, George Moore, responding to a question about how commonwealth attorneys decide where to seek the death penalty, said, "None of us like to dance on graves."

What an odd way, I thought, to end a hearing, but that was about it.

I walked out of the annex with Senator Wooton and thanked him for all his trouble in driving to Kentucky to testify on our behalf.

He said it was not a problem, and he was glad to do it.

"Is it tough," I asked, "keeping the death penalty from being reinstated in West Virginia?"

He looked at me in some surprise, and said, "I don't want to know what the popular opinion on the death penalty is in West Virginia. There is always pressure on us to reinstate it."

"It would be a real blow to us if you did. Do you think that will happen?"

"Not as long as I am chairman of the Judiciary Committee. The reinstatement bills are never called."

We both laughed lightly at the irony, shook hands, and he left.

There was now end-of-the-year fundraising to be done, preparation for the 2002 General Assembly in January, organizing volunteers once again, and on it goes.

Our theory was we were now in position for a vote on

our bills in the House and Senate Judiciary Committees because they had heard the issues and the arguments and it was time for the bills to be posted in committee for votes.

As we were getting ready for the holidays, we got a strong statement from the capitol in Frankfort. Governor Paul Patton announced he supported abolishing the death penalty for juveniles. He was no longer dancing around the issue; he was with us.

That made a difference. It could make a big difference when we got into the major struggles of the 2002 session.

We were ready to move on once again.

13

A NEW BEGINNING

Kaye had been talking to us for some time about her increasing problem of working, even part time. Her son, Brendan, was no longer a docile crawling infant, but was a hell-bent young walker, and runner. She had her hands full.

We began a search and found Mary McCarthy, whom we hired as campaign coordinator at the munificent salary of $24,000 a year plus health insurance.

Mary was a tall, thin, hyperactive lady with past careers in radio and television reporting, and always involved in a large family of parents and siblings. She knew Kentucky, a good bit about politics, was an ardent abolitionist, and a kind, nice person. We thought she would do well, and she did.

Mary soon was used to our ways and our volunteers were becoming old hands. We could be more strategic and use our forces more effectively.

We prepared for the upcoming 2002 Kentucky legislative session believing this time it would be different. We had matured. Nothing could surprise us. We had a successful interim hearing on our two major bills and this would lead to a posting and committee vote during the session.

I said these things to Pat, and he said them back to me, and we said them to our troops, and in time we came to believe. This time would be different.

Our initial strategy was to go in with more caution and concentrate on lining up the maximum support for our two bills before making any public pronouncements. Pat and I began seeing key legislators; we now had the governor's support on the juvenile death penalty abolition bill to use with Democrats.

We needed new faces to lead the cause, and while abolition was our goal, it was clear that we could find more support for the juvenile bill than for full abolition.

The Senate was less receptive to our cause than the House so we increased our attention there. Our most powerful potential ally was Senator David Karem, Democrat from Louisville. He had been majority leader before the Republicans gained control, and now he was minority leader.

Senator Karem was a big, dark-haired man who seemed always on the move. He was a respected, usually liberal voice, and favored the abolition of the death penalty. He could in theory have been a great help to us, but in practice he really wasn't. Senator Karem took his leadership role seriously and would not sponsor controversial bills, or push his fellow Democratic senators to do so because he needed them for more practical and immediate political goals. He was a vote for us, and that was about it.

Senator Karem's advice to me was, "Go find a very conservative Republican to lead the abolition cause. That's what you need." He did not suggest where such a creature might be hiding.

Another ally was Senator Gerald Neal who in the past sessions was supportive but had not been active recently because of other issues that engaged him. However, in a conversation early in 2002 he said he was ready to take a lead role on the juvenile bill. That was good news.

Gerald Neal was an organizer, a trader, a facilitator, and a very practical man trying to accomplish reachable goals. It was true that he was a liberal in a sea of fundamentalists, but he had a vote, and sometimes they needed him just as much as he needed them. He had been there for a while, and he knew how the game was played.

We welcomed Senator Neal's help and we heeded his advice not to introduce a juvenile bill in either the Senate or the

House until we had lined up as many sponsors as possible.

Unbeknownst to us, Senator Neal had a talk with Representative Robin Webb about the juvenile bill. She was not strong on abolishing the death penalty, but she told Gerald she did favor the juvenile bill, and more importantly, was willing to take a leadership role on the bill in the House. Robin Webb, like Gerald Neal, was goal-oriented. He thought she could be of enormous help in the House, and recommended that to us.

Here was a new and effective player on the scene. Pat and I welcomed her and accepted her offer. We shared our information and began working with her seeking additional sponsors in the House.

I had several opportunities for uninterrupted conversations with Robin Webb and I became one of her many admirers. She was from Grayson, Kentucky, representing Carter and Lewis counties in the northeastern mountains of Kentucky. She was independent, conservative like her district on most issues, and a fighter for better health care and health insurance for her impoverished Appalachian constituents.

Robin Webb was a good-looking woman. She was tall and slender with bangs and straight blonde hair worn to her shoulders. She grew up in Carter County on a farm without indoor plumbing, and with plenty of work. There were few sports or outdoor activities that Robin didn't like and wasn't good at. Naturally enough, she started with horses and riding. At a young age she became an expert on walking horses and qualified as a judge of livestock at the county and state fairs.

The Webbs were an interesting clan. On Robin's father's side, the generations went back to colonial days in Pennsylvania, where they'd come from Wales. They were hunters and farmers with close ties to Daniel Boone's family, which had also settled in Pennsylvania. Family stories had it that the daughter of Squire Boone (Daniel's brother) had an affair, and when it became known, the local Quaker community pressured the Boones to move on. They gathered their stock and loaded the wagons and headed for the Carolinas. Because the Boones and the Webbs were close and intermarried, the Webbs picked up and went with them. As the years passed both families explored westward and crossed the mountains into Kentucky. Along the way the Webbs picked up some Cherokee blood, and were one of the first to settle in famous Butcher Hollow. The Webbs were hunters and farmers, and then worked in the coal mines, until Robin's great grandfather broke the chain and became a preacher. He moved north to Greenup County and later into southern Ohio.

Robin's grandparents were farmers, but her father studied and became an optometrist and developed a practice in Ashland and Grayson, Kentucky, and her mother became a realtor in Grayson. Her father, Dr. Robert Webb, taught Robin to hunt and fish, and they became leading conservationists in Kentucky. Dr. Webb was a solid Eastern Kentucky Republican, and was an alternate delegate to the 1968 Republican National Convention.

Her mother, on the other hand, was a dedicated Democrat, and she was a delegate to the 1972 Democratic National Convention. Robin went with her to that convention, and she chose, with her mother, to be a Democrat. Regardless of this divergence, they were all Southern Baptists.

Education was a big thing with the Webbs. After graduating from high school Robin went to Morehead College and took pre-med courses. In the summer she worked with the men in the underground coal mines. Besides making good money she became fascinated with mining. When she returned to college she switched majors, and became an engineer. She received degrees in Mining Technology and a bachelor of science in Energy and Reclamation. After graduation she worked with a major mining company in Eastern Kentucky. With the strong encouragement of her employer, she went to law school. She studied at Chase Law School in Northern Kentucky, mostly at night, and when she graduated she passed the bar, and started practicing law.

Sports, conservation, law, mining, politics, and her two children—Robin Webb was one busy, talented, and successful lady.

In my early days with Robin Webb one thing pulled me up short. She was a handsome woman, she dressed smartly, and she was well-educated. When she spoke though, out came an Eastern Kentucky nasal twang that sounded strange to me, and seemed incongruous. I did get used to it, though.

By the third week of the legislative session Senator Neal and Representative Webb thought the time had come, and on January 22 they filed identical bills in the Senate and the House prohibiting the execution of sixteen and seventeen year olds. In the Senate it was Senate Bill 120, with Walter Blevins, Marshall Long, Ed Miller, Ernesto Scorsone, and Johnny Turner as co-sponsors. In the House, it was House Bill 447, with Tim Feeley, John Adams, Paul Bather, Scott Brinkman, Tom Burch, H. Graham, Bob Heleringer, Mary Lou Marzian, Reginald Meeks, Arnold Simpson, Kathy Stein, Susan Westrom, and Rob Wilkey as co-sponsors.

Not bad at all, I thought.

Our next goal was to get commitments of support from a majority of the members of the House and Senate Judiciary Committees, and we made steady progress. The Senate was a much taller mountain, but Senator Neal worked at it cagily.

Representative Tom Burch prepared and filed a death penalty abolition bill in the House, with Heleringer, Bather, Marzian, Meeks, Stein and Wayne as cosponsors. The filing date was February 8, and the bill was numbered HB 630.

Tom Burch was always a help to us. He was Irish Catholic, long in Democratic politics, and a representative in the legislature for many years. He was strong for the abolition of the death penalty and a strong supporter of women's rights, including abortion rights. For these views he received the support of civil liberties groups, and was unwelcome at the Knights of Columbus. His views were more liberal than those in his suburban district but he managed to win elections, even if narrowly, by out-working and out-hustling his opponents.

Representative Burch was a pale Irishman, a little pudgy,

and he talked out of the side of his mouth; and smiled a lot. From our perspective, he was there, we knew where he stood, and we could depend on him. He wanted to be, and he was, a very nice man.

Patterns developed as our lobbying techniques matured. Ideally we were able to sit down with a senator or representative and not only discuss the issues of the death penalty but gain some insight into his or her goals and philosophy, and political sensitivities.

We divided the responses we received into three categories: those who were with us or most likely would be; those who were not with us, and most likely never would be; and those in the middle about whom we couldn't be sure. After each meeting, and with the reports I received from volunteers, I entered all this information in my black book.

Rarely were we rudely received. It happened, but not often. On a few occasions we heard a definite, "Yes, I'm with you," or on the other end of the spectrum, "No, I am not going to vote for that." Most often what we heard, over and over was, "I haven't thought much about the death penalty issue before, but I'll keep an open mind and listen to the arguments..." and so forth.

Most senators and representatives love to leave you thinking they might be with you because they like you and your arguments are so good—no matter who you are or what you're touting. We volunteer lobbyists love to find support, and often we hear what we want to hear and our prognostications get rosier and rosier.

In the legislative course of any controversial bill, and certainly the abolition bills, there developed a ritual dance of sparring, in and out, back and forth, within the committees, the office cubbyholes, and over evening drinks. No one ever quite knew who was doing what to whom. If you were experienced and watched carefully, you learned you best be suspicious of everyone, and most particularly those who on the surface should be the least suspect.

I arrived home from Frankfort one afternoon to a message from Kenyon Meyer. Oral arguments before the Kentucky Supreme Court on Frank Tamme's case were set for the following Tuesday, and Kenyon would like as many people as possible to attend court and show support. We got the word out, and I looked forward to the arguments. The state was appealing the circuit court's decision granting Frank Tamme a third trial and I thought we had a good case.

We gathered in the supreme court chambers. Seeing this ornate room with its rich wall paneling to the high ceiling, I was struck with memories. This was where I had been sworn in to the practice of law and where I had argued cases that seemed very important to me at the time.

The seven judges sat on high to the left as you entered, and then there was a lower row for the clerk and other officers of the court, then the lawyers' tables and chairs at ground level, and finally a railing separating the seats for the public. On each section of paneling on the walls were oil portraits of our departed jurists, looking old and austere.

The lawyers arrived with assistants and briefcases and made the quick gestures of lightheartedness born of nervous anxiety. The clerk and interns moved with purpose readying everything for the opening of court.

I found a seat with Mary, Kaye, and Pat and looked about at the many familiar faces around us. A small frail woman in a wheelchair was brought in and positioned in front and to my left. She looked about alertly with a small sweet expression, dark eyes, but her forehead knotted up tight in expectation. Pat leaned over and said, "That's Frank Tamme's mother."

I went over, introduced myself and said hello, and she took my hand in both of hers and looked up at me seeking reassurance. I told her it would all go well, and she thanked me. I wondered if she knew of Frank's illness, but I said nothing.

The public seats were divided in half by an aisle, and whether by happenstance or by design all of our people were sitting to the left of the aisle and a growing number of pro-death penalty victims' advocates were taking seats on the right. Our glances occasionally caught one another but no sign of acknowledgment was given. Almost without exception these men and women looked angry. I wondered how we looked to them. We sat waiting for court to open.

The impressive trappings, the veneer of civility, and the rituals evolved over eons of repetition were all so familiar, but now they filled me with fear. I was afraid of these people across the aisle. I was afraid of the judges who were to decide the fate of Mrs. Tamme's son. I was as aware of the power of the state as I had been that night Harold McQueen was executed. My cry of that night was still deep inside me.

The bailiff banged his gavel, startling everyone, "Oyez, Oyez, everyone rise," and the proceedings were underway.

The commonwealth, represented by the attorney general's office, was the appellant and argued first. Then Kenyon Meyer argued for Frank Tamme, with time for rebuttals.

I thought the arguments for the state were lackluster, but over and over again the point was made that justice required finality. There had to be an end for the criminal justice system, for society, and for victims. There were, of course, a slew of cases that could be cited for that proposition. Frank Tamme had been tried and convicted twice. How many times was he to get?

Kenyon Meyer did well. He had a compelling argument on the facts as they had finally been disclosed, and his boyish sincerity and good looks didn't hurt. There were very few questions asked by any of the judges of either side, which surprised me. I gleaned nothing from these proceedings about how the judges would vote. From past experience I felt confident of two, perhaps three votes for us, but from there on I was just guessing.

When the arguments were over, we all rose, the judges filed out, and there was nothing else we could do. Mrs. Tamme was wheeled out of the courtroom, looking tired and perplexed. Once again we had to wait.

A quarter of the legislative session was now past. Tuesday lobbying and shepherding volunteers was proceeding when Pat received a call from Gerald Neal's office asking us to meet with him at ten o'clock that following morning. We rearranged things to make that possible and were there on time.

We were not the only ones invited. There were a half dozen others sitting around the table including Ed Monahan of DPA; Judy Campbell, a woman long active in politics and currently working for the Justice Cabinet; Becky Stevens of the Children's Alliance; Dr. Kerby Neill; Shelia Schuster, director of the Kentucky Psychological Association; and Jane Chiles.

Senator Neal was not there, and to those who knew him that was not a surprise. We talked and reported on what was going on and then there was a stir in the outer office. In a moment a new energy came into the room and it was Senator Neal. He was moving, he was nodding at us, and he was sorting through a stack of telephone messages he had been handed. When he was behind his desk he laid the messages down, looked up, and smiled broadly at all of us.

Gerald Neal had certainly had his share of defeats in life, but he had a way of looking like a winner. He gave the impression he knew and understood what was going on and that was a considerable asset.

"I thank all of you for coming on short notice," he said, "and I assume you all know each other." We nodded that was the case and about that time Representative Robin Webb came in, nodded to everyone, and took a seat.

Gerald Neal came around and sat on the edge of his desk and at first was smiling and then took on a very serious look.

"There is something going on," he said. "Something special is going on. I suspect you are hearing things about our death penalty bills the same way I am. There is a lot of opposition to the abolition bill, but there is also the beginning of a resonance, a resonance building in the hearts and minds..." and now Gerald Neal got a mischievous, playful smile, as he repeated slowly, "in the hearts and minds of my fellow legislators. They are having trouble with the idea of executing juveniles. Killing grown-ups doesn't bother them, but killing kids does.

"I know we were all hopeful when we started, I know I was. But now, I sense it is becoming more than that. We have the beginnings, I believe, of a real movement that can succeed, and the reason I asked you here is to say that, and to ask you if we can come together as we never have before, and concentrate on the juvenile bill, and make this movement succeed. This is going to mean less emphasis on abolishing the death penalty entirely, and it is going to require bringing in additional people and groups to work on the juvenile bill.

"Many of you in this room came together in the coalition to pass the Racial Justice Act in 1998. And while we all know that was a miracle of sorts, we also know that any good bill that passes this legislature is a miracle one way or the other. It is time for us to move again, and create another miracle.

"Look here. You psychologists know, and you tell me, that children's minds and emotions do not fully mature until they're in their twenties. We don't let them vote until they're eighteen. They can't drink legally until they're twenty-one. We know they are not fully responsible when they are sixteen and seventeen, and yet we are executing them for murder. It makes no sense."

We were looking at a man who had seen that something really could happen, and he had a plan, and he was getting up a head of steam.

"I know KCADP is out there lobbying for abolition of the death penalty. I know that the folks from Juvenile Justice and the child psychologists are deeply interested in the juvenile bill. And, of course, I know that the Department of Public Advocacy has an interest in all the death penalty bills. The questions I pose to you…are you willing to come together, form a coalition with some new folks, and set our sights to pass the juvenile bill?"

Jane Chiles responded first as a "Yes" from the Catholic Conference, and of course Becky Stevens of the Children's'

Alliance was enthusiastic, and I watched and listened as Gerald Neal drew each one of them out.

When he got to Ed Monahan of the Department of Public Advocacy, he said, "You know, we have the governor with us now, you guys should be able to go all out."

"We will," Ed responded. "I know Commissioner Ralph Kelly of Justice wants to; although we have been disappointed we haven't gotten more encouragement from the governor."

Gerald Neal's smile became very wide and he said softly, "the governor and I have been talking...and I believe, Ed, we will be getting more support from the governor."

Before Gerald Neal could continue, Ed Monahan stood up to get attention (which was unusual for him) and said, "Senator Neal, there is another aspect of the juvenile bill campaign that you may not be aware of, and that's the Larry Osborne case."

Gerald Neal spread his hands in front of him in innocence and said, "I'm not aware of it."

"It's a case of a seventeen-year-old Whitley County kid convicted of murder and sentenced to death. What it shows is that kids, or at least this kid, do not get justice. I'd like to tell you about it. It's about as bad as you can get—even for Whitley County."

Gerald Neal sat down behind his desk and Ed moved and stood so he could see all of us, and he began his tale. He spoke softly and slowly, and looked at us with large sad eyes that gave you the feeling he really meant what he said and it was something we should know.

"Right before Christmas in 1997, on December 13 to be exact, a much respected old couple, Sam and Lillian Davenport – he was a decorated Marine from World War II and she was a mother, not only to her children but to the community—these two old people were murdered in their home. Someone broke in and knocked both of them unconscious, stole stuff, and set fire to their little frame house. That night two kids, seventeen-year-old Larry Osborne and fifteen-year-old Joe Reid, were at a gathering at a girl's house not far from the Davenports and towards midnight they headed home, to Joe's house, on a borrowed motorbike.

"The two boys said that when they passed the Davenport's house on Kentucky Route 1804 they heard the sound of glass breaking coming from the house but they didn't see anybody. When they got to Joe's house Larry called his mother, Pat Osborne, and told her what he and Joe had heard, and that he was scared. She said they should call the police. Pat Osborne did call 911 and told the operator what the boys had said.

"Now, let me give you a little background," and Ed looked around at all of us in his quiet lawyerly way.

"You know, of course, that Whitley County is pretty remote and it is a violent place. In fact, at the time the Davenports were murdered there had already been six or seven murder-robberies in that area that year, and there was a lot of agitation about the fact that nobody had been caught.

"Another thing is, Larry Osborne had problems. Some of them he may not even have been aware of. For one thing, the local police had a standing theory that Larry's mother, Pat Osborne, was the ringleader of a local gang of thieves. Why they thought so I don't know, but we do know she had an IQ test of fifty-four, so it couldn't have been a very smart gang. Now, Larry had no police record, which could not be said of either his brother or his father. His father was an alcoholic who caused lots of problems, and as a matter of fact, I guess Larry was the only working and steady guy in the whole crowd.

"After Pat Osborne called the police, Officer Sam Durham went to the Davenport's house and it was then in flames. The police called Larry, his friend Joe Reid, and Larry's mother, and told them to come to the scene. They took statements and the boys gave their story of what happened as I've outlined.

"For whatever reason, the police decided to concentrate on Larry Osborne and Joe Reid as the culprits, and they targeted fifteen-year-old Joe Reid to be interrogated. They brought Joe in to the station and questioned him at length on December 14 and again on December 16. Each time he was questioned, Joe Reid was by himself. There was no family member with him, or a lawyer, or any grown-up, except the police. Joe Reid consistently told the police officers the same story. He said the two of them had left the girl's house on the motorbike, heard the glass breaking as they were passing the Davenport's house, went to Joe Reid's house, and Larry called his mother.

"The police brought Joe back to the station again on December 31, New Year's Eve. Now they told him that he was a suspect in the murders. But they also told him that he might be able to get out of a lot of trouble if he told them the truth. This time a civilian polygraph operator, Richard Kurtz, who worked with the state police, was brought in, and he and a detective over a four-hour period interrogated the fifteen-year-old. In the process of interrogation they told Joe Reid all the facts that the police investigation had uncovered. They drew a diagram of the house, showing where the bodies were found. They showed the boy photographs the police had taken of the scene and gave him a narrative of how they thought the robbery and murders had been committed. The murderer had broken out a security light in the rear of the house, dragged a bench around to the side of the house, smashed a window, and climbed in. But Joe Reid stuck to his story that he and Larry Osborne had nothing to do with these murders.

"Then, Richard Kurtz gave Joe Reid a polygraph test and when it was over he told him he had failed it. Under Kentucky State Police procedures this interrogation was recorded on video camera, but after the polygraph test the camera was turned off, and it remained off for approximately forty minutes. When it was turned back on Officer Gary Lane could be heard telling Joe Reid they were going to help him. Joe Reid then said, in response to questions, that Larry Osborne was the murderer. He looked at the officers and asked, 'Is this going to get me out of all this stuff?'

"A few days later the police and the prosecutor took Joe Reid before the Whitley County Grand Jury, and while he told the grand jury a somewhat different story than he had told the police on

New Year's Eve, it still ended with Larry Osborne as the murderer.

"The grand jury indicted Larry Osborne for the murder of Sam and Lillian Davenport, and indicted his mother, Pat Osborne, with complicity to commit murder.

"Other than this statement of Joe Reid there was no evidence that Larry Osborne had anything to do with the murders. The police stated that small shards of glass found on Larry Osborne's trousers showed he had broken the window to get into the Davenport's house. When the glass particles were examined in the state lab they did not match the Davenport's window glass. The police stated that a witness saw Larry Osborne at the Davenport's house before the murders, but the witness's description of the person nowhere resembled Larry Osborne.

"But trial preparations proceeded. Early that summer Joe Reid went to visit friends in Tennessee and while swimming in a lake he accidentally drowned. In the months before Joe Reid died, Larry Osborne's defense lawyer had not been permitted by the court to take Joe Reid's deposition or in any way to examine or cross-examine Joe Reid on why he had changed his story of what had happened.

"In any event the prosecution took the case to trial with little evidence except Joe Reid's grand jury testimony and they persuaded the trial judge to let them read Joe Reid's statement to the jury, and other than object, there was little the defense could do to rebut the accusation.

"The judge let the case go to the jury. The jury found Larry Osborne guilty of murder, and he was sentenced to be executed." As I looked around, Gerald Neal was nodding his head back and forth sideways in sadness, and someone in the group said, "Oh, my God."

Gerald Neal stood up again. "This will be our attack mode. Two pronged. First," and he raised one arm high, finger extended, "We should not be killing kids. It is morally wrong, and they're too young to be held fully accountable. And second," he raised his other arm with one finger extended, "When we do try kids in death penalty cases, they don't get justice."

We all nodded our heads in agreement and the senator looked at Robin Webb and said, "Please excuse me, Representative Webb, I have been doing all the talking. Tell us what you think." Robin Webb was not one who required center stage and she had not minded sitting there and taking it all in. She responded without getting up, "Senator Neal, I could not be more pleased in hearing your enthusiasm for the juvenile bill. I think you are absolutely right that now is a time when we have a great opportunity. I feel it in the House, and I can report to you that we now have ten solid commitments from Judiciary Committee members, which is a clear majority. We are ready to go for a vote in Judiciary. I am also confident that when we get out of Judiciary we will have the votes to carry on the House floor. I haven't heard of anyone planning to derail us once we're out of committee.

"I suggest it may be best for us to push first in the House and try to come out of the House with enough momentum that it will help overcome the hurdles in the Senate."

"All RIGHT!" Gerald Neal trumpeted. "Let's do it."

Neal then looked at me and Pat and said, "Can you get up a pamphlet, like some of the others you've done, but just about this kid, Larry Osborne—with just the facts—hard hitting? We'll spread it all over the capitol."

Pat and I agreed. I headed for Ed Monahan to get a copy of his fact sheet on Larry Osborne. I was plotting out in my mind the headline: "Juvenile Sentenced to be Executed on Testimony of Dead Fifteen-Year-Old."

Gerald Neal was excited and he continued talking, addressing each of the constituencies sitting around the table; contact this senator, that representative, get cosponsors, plan a demonstration, a news conference, and so on.

Everything had suddenly changed. Gerald Neal, Ed Monahan, and Robin Webb had lit a fire.

.

14

POWER

The tempo quickened. You could sense new energy in the campaign. That weekend we prepared our materials and schedules for the Tuesday-Wednesday-Thursday volunteers, and I designed a pamphlet on the Larry Osborne case, letter size, front and back. After printing, the page was folded in half, the picture of Larry on the front page and some headlines, and the full story on the inside and the back.

Pat did the graphics on his computer and when he was finished it looked both official and authoritative. We made a couple hundred copies to be distributed by volunteers starting on Tuesday. This is the front page:

SHOULD KENTUCKY KILL CHILDREN?

SHOULD A SEVENTEEN-YEAR OLD BOY BE EXECUTED ON THE UNCORROBORATED TESTIMONY OF A FIFTEEN-YEAR OLD WHO IS DEAD

This boy is in a cell on Kentucky's Death Row

A b o l i t i o n   N o w

Kentucky Coalition to Abolish the Death Penalty • PO Box 3092 • Louisville Kentucky • (502) 585-2895 • www.kcadp.org • kcadp@earthlink.net

For the campaign's new emphasis, I needed to revise the instructions for volunteers, stressing the juvenile bill. I was having trouble with this and I said to Pat, "Let's talk," and we found some time.

The abolition of the death penalty was important because it is a moral abomination for the state to kill. State executions condoned violence as a solution, and we believed encouraged acts of violence. This was the heart and soul of the abolition campaign, and my participation in it.

The politicians were beginning to feel foolish and embarrassed by the practice of killing juveniles, and the rationale for ending it was that juveniles were not mature enough to recognize the full consequences of their acts. This was an argument akin to the one for not executing the mentally retarded. Implied in all this was the recognition that if in fact the juvenile were intellectually and emotionally mature (or the individual were not mentally retarded), it was okay to execute them. From my view those arguments were meaningless; it was not okay.

But if we could pass the juvenile bill it would be a step forward, and it might make the next step that much easier. We needed a win.

I found, to no surprise, Pat had these same reservations and conflicting emotions. We talked it out, and agreed it would be foolish for us not to go ahead. We recognized that the conflict between pragmatism and morality in this instance was not a healthy one, but it was curable in the long run.

We met often with Robin Webb and Gerald Neal and they gave high priority in their schedules to the juvenile bill. We discussed timing. We needed to get out of the House Judiciary Committee as soon as possible. Then it was on to the House floor for the required three readings and a prompt vote, and hopefully passage with a strong enough majority to take us to the Senate with publicity and momentum. We needed time in the Senate to muster our growing support and to let Gerald Neal do his thing. As a session moved on and time began to get short, things had a way of getting out of hand.

We concluded we needed our bills to be posted in the House Judiciary Committee by the committee's second regular Wednesday meeting in February, and no later than the third. It was time to call on the chair, Representative Gross Lindsay.

The question we raised was who should go visit the chairman, and what approach to take?

Robin Webb advised, "I think it is best if I work in the background right now, and not irritate the chairman. So, I suggest that you, as citizen volunteers, go see Gross Lindsay and ask him to call the abolition bills. I wouldn't single out the juvenile bill right now; I'd ask him for both bills. You can tell him we have the committee votes to get the bills out, and see what he says. That way if he gets upset, it's you he's upset with, and I'm free to talk to him later."

We followed her advice. Pat, Jane Chiles, and I went to see him. It would have been good to have Ed Monahan, but he worked for state government and would shy away from such a meeting.

Jane Chiles had the best rapport with the chairman and she got an appointment for Tuesday at 9:00 in the morning. We were to meet in the lobby on the third floor of the annex outside Lindsay's office shortly before nine, and that was about all the planning we needed.

On Tuesday morning the reception area was busy with lobbyists, and a contingent of several dozen senior citizens wearing large buttons, "Vote NO on House Bill..." They were being led and given directions by a woman with a piercing high voice. I had no idea how this house bill was threatening seniors, but when some of them recognized me as one of their own, we smiled and I gave them a raised power fist and said, "Go for it!" They seemed pleased.

Pat and Jane and I waited for a few minutes and then Jackie, the receptionist, nodded to us, gave us security badges, and smiled, "Representative Lindsay can see you now."

The offices for the legislators are arranged in clusters. We walked down the main hall and entered Gross Lindsay's cluster that had a small reception area, two desks for legislative assistants, and a couple of chairs for guests. An attendant talking on the phone waved for us to proceed to the small hallway in the back that led to four offices. One was marked "Representative Gross Lindsay," and we entered. He rose and greeted each of us with a smile and a handshake, and the light banter began.

"Well," he said, "you're about your good works early this morning."

"Yes indeed," Jane Chiles answered, giving Gross Lindsay the full treatment of her radiant smile. "I don't think any of us can get ahead of you though, Representative Lindsay, I hear you're up at five walking the capitol grounds."

Lindsay smiled, "I do try and get out there and get the old bones moving."

So we sat and smiled at each other envisioning Representative Lindsay's old bones moving at five in the morning.

Pat spoke up. "How do you see the session going, Representative Lindsay?"

"You know," he said, looking at us one at a time, "I wish you'd call me Gross."

Jane responded, "That's nice of you, and Gross it will be."

Gross then leaned back in his chair, put his fingers together in front of his chin and pondered Pat's question. We remained silent.

"This session is one of the gol-darndest I guess I've ever seen. Everyone and his cousin are running for governor, and that makes it hard to get anything done. You cannot imagine all we've got on our docket. The Judiciary Committee gets all the tough stuff that leadership doesn't know what to do with. And I read all this stuff – I have to. A lot of it's crazy."

"You were wise to hold a hearing on the death penalty bills in the interim," Jane said, "so we won't have to take up additional committee time when the abolition bills are posted.

The posting of our two bills, House Bill 630, the abolition bill, and House Bill 447, the juvenile bill, is what we'd like to talk with you about."

"There's a surprise," Gross Lindsay said with a laugh, and he tapped his desk and leaned back slowly, staring at us.

"We have the votes in your committee, and we have the votes on the House floor to pass the juvenile bill, but the session is moving along, and, of course, we're anxious to get moving."

"Of course you are," Representative Lindsay replied, nodding his head, looking steadily at the three of us.

"Almost 80 percent of Kentuckians are opposed to killing kids, and 54 percent now favor life in prison over the death penalty," Pat put in.

"We have, as you may have noticed" (and here Pat smiled), "been lobbying these bills with volunteers from all over the state, and particularly lobbying the members of your Judiciary Committee."

Representative Lindsay again nodded. "Yes, I have noticed," he said.

As Pat talked, Representative Lindsay watched him without making any other sign.

"House Bill 312, the juvenile bill, has gathered support that, frankly, even surprised us. Representative Robin Webb has gotten a large number of cosponsors for her bill and more and more legislators are telling us that while they are not ready to come with us on abolition, they will vote for the juvenile bill because they don't think we should be killing kids."

Representative Lindsay continued to stare, his chin deep in his collar, eyeing Pat over his half-glasses.

I could tell Lindsay's lack of a real response was getting to Pat, but he kept his voice and manner as positive as he could.

The three of us sat and waited while Gross Lindsay sat there and studied us. His eyebrows first were tight together in concentration, and then raised high as if in amazement. He did this several times and fiddled with something on his desk.

"In my experience," he said, "kids sixteen and seventeen years old can be just as bad and mean as any grown-up I've ever encountered."

He leaned over his desk looking at us.

This time Jane Chiles spoke. "Will you please post these two bills, so the representatives can have their say, and the legislative process can go forward?"

"You know, Jane," and now Representative Lindsay's slightly skewered smile returned, "these committee members don't always tell me the same thing they tell you. A lot of these people ask me not to call these bills."

Jane's smile never faded as she nodded and listened. After a moment she said, "Will you post these two bills on your docket?"

"Well, we'll see."

Rep. Lindsay began to shift in his chair and he picked up some papers on his desk and was preparing for other work.

I then spoke up for the first time since the hellos. "Can you tell us when we will know?"

He looked at me and said, "We'll see."

The three of us went to the basement cafeteria for coffee and looked at each other.

"That was about as non-productive a meeting as you could have." I was wondering if we should have made more about his implied commitment during the interim meeting, and I raised the question.

"No, I don't think so," Pat responded. "What I think we need to do now is to go back to leadership and see if they will move Gross. But first, let's report to Gerald and Robin, and see what they say."

This we did, and both Robin and Gerald thought that was the thing to do, and we planned accordingly.

One of the things I particularly enjoyed at this stage of our politicking was getting to know Gerald Neal. He was a Democrat from Louisville, the only African American in the Kentucky Senate, and I guessed he was in his early fifties. He was a handsome man, standing about five foot ten, and dapper. Besides being a senator, he was a lawyer and a businessman. He could be brusque, he could be charming, he could be thoughtful, and almost always he was focused and determined.

Occasionally we had a chance to talk, and he liked talking about his family, particularly telling stories about his father, Sterling Neal.

Sterling Neal had been a union man. He was a leader and creator in whatever he did, and one of his accomplishments was integrating Local 236 of the United Farm Equipment Workers, representing workers at the International Harvester plant. The plant came to Louisville in the late 1940s to take advantage of the cheap, non-union, local labor, and the UFEW changed all that. Through Sterling Neal's efforts the Local was not only integrated, but its black and white members worked together for improvements for all the workers in the plant. In the 1940s and 1950s that was rarely heard of in the South. Gerald Neal was very proud and respectful of his mother and father, and what they had accomplished.

We got in to see Greg Stumbo, the Majority Leader in the House, and his wife and new baby were in his office, and they were both quite beautiful.

He took us into a side room and listened to what we had to say. By now he was aware of the progress being made on the juvenile bill. He would not say he was with us, but it appeared he was struggling with the idea of executing children.

He agreed after a bit that leadership in the House would discuss our bills, and that he would talk to Gross Lindsay.

It was hard to know what that meant, but at least we had gotten his attention for a time.

Getting to see the Speaker of the House, Jody Richards, was easier because he was more accessible, and he and Jane were thick. He patiently listened to our pitch, and he knew generally what we were doing, and readily agreed he would speak to Gross Lindsay about our bills.

Of course, there was no way for us to know what these guys would say to Gross Lindsay. They knew what we wanted them to say, and we had to hope for the best. As we were leaving Richard's office I was last in line and Jody took my arm and held me back while the others left the room.

He said to me, "I want you to know the work you are doing in this cause is admirable, and I admire you and your work enormously."

He squeezed my arm as he was saying this and then led me out to join Pat and Jane.

I mumbled thanks, and as the three of us walked off I felt pretty sure the Speaker's stroking my ego was not a good sign of what was going to happen to our bills. I did not say anything about this to Pat and Jane, but I was not encouraged.

That Saturday I took the day off. There was too much going on in my head, and I felt the edges of a beginning sadness. A cold February rain was falling. I went down in the basement and got out the small and large bait boxes and sat on the basement step under the light and poked around with my fishing tackle. The light crank bait for bass fishing I knew well. I had used many of them for years. The dry and wet flys in their boxes were much newer to me and came with fewer memories.

I loved to fish, ever since my dad first took me as a kid. I particularly liked to fish for small-mouth bass. I'd been fly fishing for only a couple of years and as I got better I found it wonderful fun. Fishing brings me a sense of peace and excitement in wild and beautiful settings that is a joy unlike any other sport or outdoor experience I've had. It is very special.

That evening Stephanie and I went to a movie, and when we got home there were three messages, and soon my head was back in the campaign.

We watched the agenda for the Wednesday Judiciary Committee meeting when it was posted on Monday, and House Bills 447 and 630 were not on it.

We went to the ten committed votes we had in the

committee and encouraged them to talk to other committee members and to tell Gross Lindsay they were ready to vote on our bills. It was difficult to judge their enthusiasm, but they all said they would.

We continued with our volunteers to seek cosponsors for our two bills. The reception we received on the juvenile bill was mostly favorable. The flyer we handed out on the Larry Osborne case was very effective. The facts surrounding his trial and conviction were hard for anyone to believe.

We made a number of attempts to reach the governor to ask him to help with Gross Lindsay. We never got to him directly, but we talked to several of his top assistants. We were invariably told they would see that the governor knew of our problem, and they were confident he would help us. All we could do was wait and watch.

At our next meeting with Robin and Gerald, Robin said she would now make her move and talk directly to the chairman about calling our two bills. Robin Webb was not on the Judiciary Committee but she and Gross Lindsay had worked together on issues and she thought they had a good rapport.

"If I really ask Gross, I believe he will call my bill," she said. "At least I hope so."

She didn't report any progress, and we assumed there wasn't any.

We continued putting on pressure every way we knew. Time was running short.

A day or two later, Gerald Neal said to us, and he was upset: "You know what? Let's have a press conference, right before the Wednesday Judiciary Committee meeting, and tell the world Gross Lindsay won't call the juvenile bill, and let the world ask him why.

"We'll get our legislative supporters and all your volunteers together and have a big press conference. If quiet pressure doesn't work on Gross Lindsay, let's see what public pressure does. We are entitled to a vote on the juvenile bill in committee, and no chairman has the right to deny us that vote. That will be our message."

If Gerald Neal were not angry he would never have suggested such a course because he preferred to work behind the scenes. But he was mad, and he was serious.

The press conference was scheduled for the next Wednesday, before the last Judiciary Committee meeting of February.

That morning was cold and the roads were icy but we filled the conference room on the third floor of the capitol with about seventy-five supporters, and there was good press and TV coverage. We furnished the media with background information and left all the speaking to the legislators.

Gerald Neal began at the podium. He welcomed the crowd and the press, and gave a review of the juvenile bill abolishing the death penalty for sixteen and seventeen year olds.

He stated the bills had majority support in both the House and the Senate but had languished for more than a month in the House and Senate Judiciary Committees.

"We have polls, we have studies, we have numerous editorials saying this is the right thing to do. At a time when we properly condemn the medieval treatment of women and children in other parts of the world, how can we condone by inaction the barbaric practice of executing our children?" Neal spoke with increasing emotion and tension in his voice, looking directly into the cameras; his voice was sad, at times angry, but always passionate. Every word he spoke was meant for the ears of the chairmen of the Judiciary Committees, Representative Gross Lindsay and Senator Bob Stivers.

When Robin Webb took the podium she said right off that she was frustrated, and she looked it.

"On the twenty-third of January," she announced in a strong voice, "I stood before you and declared that the execution of youthful offenders in this state was on trial; however, we can't even get an arraignment, let alone a trial date.

"The United States is the only industrialized nation where

the practice of killing children is accepted and actually carried out. We share this disturbing distinction with countries such as Iran and Pakistan, one of whom has been declared one of the 'Axis of Evil' by our president."

Many of these declarations received cheers and applause and the tension and restlessness of the crowd was strong in the room.

Robin Webb concluded, "For one last time we call upon Representative Lindsay and Senator Stivers to do the right thing. Let the people's representatives' voices be heard."

The reporters asked questions of the individual representatives and senators, then the TV cameras were put away and it was over. We would see what effect it had.

There was good coverage on TV that night and in the papers the next morning. Joseph Gerth of *The Courier Journal* interviewed both Gross Lindsay and Bob Stivers. He reported Lindsay saying he is "still studying the House version of the bill" filed more than a month ago. He refused to say when he would decide whether to allow a vote. Gerth further reported Stivers said few of his committee members have even talked to him about the vote.

It did not appear we had budged a soul. Our volunteers continued to come, and mostly they were angry.

If we didn't get our bills posted and voted at the next meeting of the House Judiciary Committee, Wednesday, March 6, it was over. There would not be time after that to make it through the House and the Senate

We met that Monday and there was nothing more we could think to do. Robin said she had a meeting scheduled with Gross Lindsay on Tuesday morning and she would make her last pitch.

This she did. And she called us together Wednesday morning. Leaning against her desk, her hands clenched tightly in front of her, she said simply, "It is not going to happen."

She stood fixed for a moment and then moved away.

"I'm sorry, but it's over." Her back was to us, and her hands had gone to her face.

We watched for a moment, and as we left each of the three of us spoke in turn. I said, "Thank you, Robin. We'll be back."

We had been doing this for so long we didn't know how to stop. Volunteers continued to come and we sent them to see their legislators. We watched the concluding weeks as the Democratic-controlled House and the Republican-controlled Senates squabbled over the biennial budget submitted by a Democratic governor.

The Democrats had run things for a long time, and were used to having their way, with a fair degree of civility. The Republicans were unaccustomed to power, and civility played little role during their learning process. It was basically a mess, and ended in a stalemate.

Pat and I observed all this and were having coffee in the cafeteria when Jane Chiles came in and spied us. She got her coffee and sat down. Without any greetings or small talk, she said, "You know what I think we should do?" We listened. "I think we should go calling on Gross Lindsay."

I will say frankly, that was about the last thing on my mind.

"Why not?" she asked. "He has given us the shaft, and he knows it, and we know it. Why shouldn't we go see him, and talk about the next legislative session? Why should we just go away and let him off the hook? Let's go bother him."

As I listened I thought that made a lot of sense. It surely was better than sitting around. Let's go and let him know we survived, and we want to know what he's up to next.

Pat started smiling, and he agreed.

Jane said she would make the appointment, and we asked her to be our spokesperson as usual. The aim of our meeting, assuming we got an appointment, was to see if we could get a vote commitment for the next session. Jane and Pat would lead the discussion and be the "good cops," and if they ran into a stonewall, I got the role of "bad cop." Nothing new there.

Gross Lindsay did agree to meet with us, and we found a time we could all make it, at 11:00 a.m. on Wednesday.

We gathered in his office and Jane began to spread her charm. The words came to me, "It seems to me, I've heard that song before."

Jane said that now that the session was over for our issues, we wanted to talk to him about where we go from here. We recognize, she said most graciously, the heavy responsibility of a committee chairman who had to take account not only of the merits of a pending bill and the ambitions of its sponsors, but also the wishes and fears of the other committee members, the party leadership, and, of course, the House membership as a whole.

Jane went on with this quite adroitly and she had the chairman's full attention. He listened and watched us, his eyes narrow, and his nose squinted, while he rubbed the back of his pink bald head gently with both hands.

Jane moved to the subject of our abolition bills and how we appreciated the fact we had a hearing during the interim, but having a hearing without a vote was about as exciting and as productive as, and she paused and smiled and said, "You know the old expression – kissing your sister."

I don't know what image that brought in the chairman's mind but he began readjusting himself in his chair and he wasn't smiling.

"Representative Lindsay," Jane concluded, "In the next session we ask that our abolition bills have a hearing and a vote."

The chairman began to shuffle stuff on his desk, and then began responding to the earlier parts of Jane's comments.

"You are right; it is not easy being a committee chairman. Best I can tell I seem to make everyone mad." He paused and laughed out loud. And we, like idiots, laughed with him.

"I do have to be mindful of the wishes of my committee members and the party leadership, and of course the whole House. It is a three-cornered stool. And we do look carefully at every bill, and I think we clean up a lot of stuff. We prevent a lot of problems."

Then there was silence and he hadn't answered Jane's request for a hearing and a vote, and she went back at it.

"I need to ask you again, Gross, will you give our abolition bills a vote in the next session?"

He couldn't avoid it now. He shook his old bald head back and forth as he said, "I can't promise you I'll do anything in the next session. Who knows what will be going on? I can't tell you one way or another. I'm certainly not going to promise you anything."

Now there was more silence. I thought it might be time for the bad cop, and Jane and I exchanged glances.

"Mr. Chairman…Gross…" I began, "let me just say a few things about the abolition campaign. We believe in our political system, and we believe in the committee system in the legislature. We wouldn't be here if we didn't. You know, most of us are just volunteers. We are doing this simply because we believe that Kentucky will be better off, will be a less violent state, if we abolish the death penalty."

I was about to continue and he interrupted. "Hell, I know that. You even wrote a book, and you came to see me in my office and gave me a copy of your book. I took that book home with me and I read the preface, and that was enough, and I put it away." And he laughed out loud, and we, again like idiots, laughed with him.

I don't know if I had more of an edge in my voice, but I continued.

"We are going throughout the state giving talks and holding forums and debates, and the more we raise questions about the death penalty the more the people listen and express their own doubts about whether killing people is the right thing to do.

"In our meetings, Gross, invariably someone will ask, 'Will we get a vote on our bill in the legislature?' and, of course, I have to answer that I don't know.

"Then they will ask, 'Why should we do all this

campaigning if we are never going to get a vote?' And, finally, they ask, 'Why can't we get a vote?'"

"I do not know the answer to this question, and so, Gross, I ask you, why won't you give us a vote?"

War had been declared. Gross Lindsay's face became crimson. He rose out of his chair and leaned across his desk towards me. Banging his fist on the desk, he announced, "I don't have to tell you why I do anything. I don't owe you, or anyone else, any explanation for what I do."

He stared at me, his mouth open, the veins at his temple pulsed wildly, two steel gray eyes burned holes through me.

We were startled into silence. Slowly the chairman sat down, still furious.

In my mind I tried to find a way to suggest that public officials did have a responsibility of explanation for their actions, a way that wouldn't send the chairman back to the ceiling, but I could find none.

I said nothing and the four of us sat in silence. It was now clear what we were talking about was power. This was not about principle, the committee system, or representative government. The chairman had an opinion, and he had the power. Period.

There was a bit more small talk in which I didn't participate, and we left.

We looked at each other a few minutes later over a cup of coffee. "Well, there it is. Now the question is, how do we get rid of a chairman?" We were not the first to ask that question, but none of us had the answer.

15

THE LAST LOBBY

After the confrontation with Chairman Lindsay there was no wind left in our sails. The volunteers were no longer encouraged and the campaign for 2002 wound down. I assumed we were at the lowest of a low ebb and I was mistaken. The Kentucky Supreme Court handed down a decision on Frank Tamme's right for a new trial. It was seven to nothing against him.

I have been surprised many times at court decisions, but this one was a stunner. It seemed so obvious that Frank Tamme was innocent and never had a fair trial. My conviction was not shared by the seven justices.

There were two concurring opinions written, and different reasons expressed for overruling Judge Noble's circuit court ruling giving Frank Tamme a new trial. The majority view was that Judge Noble had found that the new evidence she had heard could "reasonably" result in a different jury verdict. The supreme court stated the correct standard was that there had to be a "reasonable certainty" of a different jury verdict.

The judges clearly had decided to bring it all to an end, and they did.

The decision was an enormous blow to everyone involved, Frank's mother, Father Dick Sullivan, attorney Kenyon Meyer, and all of us. And, the struggle was finally over for Frank Tamme. Sister Chris reported that Frank simply gave up. There was nothing left he could find to fight for. In a short time he had to be moved, because of illness, from death row at the Kentucky State Penitentiary to the Kentucky State Reformatory, and then to an Oldham County hospital, where he succumbed to hepatitis. He died before he could be executed.

Think as I might, there was no way to find solace in the saga of Frank Tamme, except perhaps that it was over.

It was the last week of the session and when I met Mary at the office she had a message. A nun from Northern Kentucky had called and said she had an appointment with Representative Joe Fischer, and she hoped I would go with her. The meeting was at Saint Walburg Convent.

I did not want to go. Joe Fischer was a lost cause for us, and it was a long drive to the convent.

On the other hand, the sister was a fine and faithful volunteer, and was determined to bring Representative Fischer, who was Catholic, into our fold. If she was going to take the time and make the effort, so should I. She gave me directions and I said I'd be there.

It was a beautiful almost spring day and I enjoyed the drive. The convent was a group of old brick buildings on a lovely rise very near the Ohio River. I found the office and was greeted, and we talked and waited until Joe Fischer arrived. We were then shown to a small old fashioned sitting room where we sat in antique chairs and pretended we were comfortable.

Representative Fischer impressed me as someone who was not all that comfortable in his own skin. He never seemed quite at ease. He was small and thin, with a sharp, bony face, but he smiled a lot.

I sat quietly as the determined nun began reciting all the moral and practical reasons we should abolish the death penalty. I noticed that Joe Fischer was holding, and occasionally glanced at, a bunch of notepaper in his hand. When she had finished, he glanced again at his notes, and said:

"It is important that we have laws that protect innocent life in the womb and I have supported every pro-life piece of legislation in the general assembly. The pope has said, and here he held up his notes he'd been referring to, "that the state has the authority to protect society, and that includes executions, which the state may carry out under the authority of God. I am not for abolition. I am not for the juvenile bill. You take a life, you give a life." And then he just threw in, "I'm not for gun control, either." He nodded his head and added seriously, "You look at the cities with the most guns—they are the safest."

I was numb. I sat silently as the sister responded to him point by point. She explained to him that while the pope did agree the state had the authority to execute, the pope further said that in modern society executions were no longer necessary to protect the public, and therefore should not be used.

Their increasingly obtuse debate, and recognizing there was no way the pope could be totally against the death penalty without damning seventeen hundred years of church history, led me into a morass of melancholy. Their talk became a distant backdrop to my thoughts roaming through those last months, and a growing wish to be rid of it all began to take over. What I really wanted was to go fishing.

I was brought back to immediacy when the sister, now standing, put her hand on my arm. "It is time to go. Representative Fischer has another meeting and so do I."

I looked up to the face of Representative Fischer, still sitting across from me, and apparently still carefully studying his notes.

I started to rise, but he reached out and stopped me by touching my knee. For the first time in the meeting he was looking me directly in the face, his eyes catching mine straight on. He leaned forward slightly and speaking softly, he said, "Let me tell you something." He paused. "I think you are going to get this done. I think you are going to end up abolishing the death penalty." He withdrew his hand and looked away, ending in a steady flat tone: "I'm just not going to help you."

We left, and the legislative session was over, and we were none too sure who was going to help us.

The case of young Larry Osborne was still pending and

because of the hearsay evidence admitted in his trial the supreme court had set aside his death penalty conviction, and his attorneys were preparing for a new trial. All of their efforts to get a change in venue and a change in trial judges were for naught so they faced, once more, a trial in a very hostile environment.

We encouraged our local supporters to attend the trial to support Larry. His counsel, Gail Robinson, was very worried about the trial because even though the damaging testimony of the dead fifteen year old, Joe Reid, couldn't be put into evidence, it was apparent many people in town thought Larry Osborne had committed the murders, and the prosecuting attorney was determined to get a death sentence.

The trial came on with the same judge but a new jury, and Larry Osborne took the stand and told the story he had told from the very beginning: he had not had anything to do with the two murders.

When they were through, the judge submitted the case to the jury, and in fairly short order the jury came back with a verdict. They found Larry Osborne "NOT GUILTY." The young man walked out of the Whitley County courthouse a dazed, but free man, and there was exultation.

All was not lost.

EPILOGUE

I did go fishing. The sound of the water lapping against the boat, the smells in the air, the occasional tug on my line, brought some serenity.

But then I had to do some deciding. What to do? Should I give up? Should all of us? I knew Pat wouldn't.

I could see how different my perspective was now, compared to three years ago when we began. Then it was filled with all sorts of possibilities. Now it was clouded with very real impossibilities.

How naive I had been. I wondered about that, and about all the things I had learned. They sure didn't seem to help much. I picked up my book, *The Second Grave*, and thumbed through it, and then set it aside.

One thing clearly was not changed. I still could not tolerate the fact that Kentucky kills people. It was indefensible, an abomination.

I gathered our crew and we talked. We began to outline a new campaign. Gradually we forgot the defeats—not entirely— but enough to give room for new energy and new hope.

I continue to be amazed at the workings of this world, but I decided it is simply better to believe that if you keep after it, good things will eventually happen. I believe this, and off we go again.